RAND Center for Corporate Ethics and Governance

Fair Value Accounting, Historical Cost Accounting, and Systemic Risk

Policy Issues and Options for Strengthening Valuation and Reducing Risk

Michael D. Greenberg, Eric Helland, Noreen Clancy, James N. Dertouzos

Supported by the Goldman Sachs Global Markets Institute

The research described in this report was supported in part by the Goldman Sachs Global Markets Institute, with additional support from the generosity of RAND's donors and by the fees earned on client-funded research, and was conducted in the RAND Center for Corporate Ethics and Governance, a part of the RAND Institute for Civil Justice.

Library of Congress Control Number: 2013950607

ISBN: 978-0-8330-8212-1

The RAND Corporation is a nonprofit institution that helps improve policy and decisionmaking through research and analysis. RAND's publications do not necessarily reflect the opinions of its research clients and sponsors.

Support RAND—make a tax-deductible charitable contribution at www.rand.org/giving/contribute.html

RAND® is a registered trademark.

RAND OFFICES
SANTA MONICA, CA • WASHINGTON, DC
PITTSBURGH, PA • NEW ORLEANS, LA • JACKSON, MS • BOSTON, MA
DOHA, QA • CAMBRIDGE, UK • BRUSSELS, BE
www.rand.org

Preface

Fair value accounting (FVA) refers to the practice of updating the valuation of assets or securities on a regular basis, ideally by reference to current prices for similar assets or securities established in the context of a liquid market. Fair value accounting is typically distinguished from *historical cost accounting* (HCA), which instead records the value of an asset as the price at which it was originally purchased. For decades, policymakers and professional experts have debated the relative merits of FVA and HCA and the quality of the information that each approach provides to investors and other key users of financial statements. In the wake of the 2008 financial crisis, conflicting arguments have been made about the contributions of valuation approaches in triggering the crisis. Critics have raised basic questions about the appropriateness of FVA methods, even as advocates pointed out that greater transparency in asset pricing and balance sheets ought to help protect against risk and speculative bubbles.

The purpose of this report is to investigate and clarify the relationship between these two accounting approaches and systemic risk to the financial system. Specifically, the report examines the risk implications of FVA and HCA in the various situations in which each is used; assesses the role that these accounting approaches have played historically in financial crises, including the 2008 financial crisis, the savings and loan crisis of the 1980s, and the less developed country (LDC) debt crisis of the 1970s; and explores insights about systemic risk that can be gleaned from better understanding the accounting approaches.

This study was funded with support from the Goldman Sachs Global Markets Institute, with additional support from the pooled resources of the RAND Center for Corporate Ethics and Governance. This report should be of interest to policymakers, regulators, financial services executives, accounting professionals and standard-setters, members of the business community, and other stakeholders with broad interests in accounting standards, valuation, risk management, systemic risk, and the global banking system.

The RAND Center for Corporate Ethics and Governance

The RAND Center for Corporate Ethics and Governance is committed to improving public understanding of corporate ethics, law, and governance and to identifying specific ways in which businesses can operate ethically, legally, and profitably. The center's work is supported by contributions from private-sector organizations and individuals with interests in research on these topics.

The center is part of the RAND Institute for Civil Justice, which is dedicated to improving the civil justice system by supplying policymakers and the public with rigorous, nonpartisan research. Its studies identify trends in litigation and inform policy choices concerning liability, compensation, regulation, risk management, and insurance.

Questions or comments about this report should be sent to the project leader, Michael Greenberg (at michaelg@rand.org). For more information on the RAND Center for Corporate Ethics and Governance, see http://www.rand.org/jie/cceg or contact the director (cceg@rand.org).

Contents

Figures and Tables

Figures

Tables

Glossary

Contagion. The transmission of financial risk across institutions or market sectors. Can sometimes occur in the absence of direct counterparty contractual commitments between the parties.

Counterparty contractual commitment. An agreement regarding a financial transaction between two parties. The two parties on the opposite sides of the transaction are said to be "counterparties."

Fundamental value. The discounted present value of a future stream of payments associated with an asset.

Gambling for resurrection. A situation in which a financial institution at risk of failure pursues a high-risk, high-return investment strategy in an attempt to retain or regain its solvency.

Illiquidity. A condition in which a financial asset cannot be readily converted into cash because of thinly traded markets and/or a lack of buyers with sufficient cash in hand to pay the fundamental value of the asset (given that "fundamental value" is the net present value of the future stream of returns associated with the asset).

Liquidity pricing. Valuation of an asset based on degree of liquidity in a thinly traded market, rather than on the asset's future earning power.

Liquidity pricing model. An economic model that seeks to explain the influence of valuation accounting on contagion of risk across financial institutions, under conditions of market illiquidity.

Mark to market. The most basic form of FVA, which involves assigning a value to an asset based on the publicly quoted price for the same asset trading on an exchange under the conditions of a liquid market.

Mark to model. A semi-pejorative expression describing FVA methods that apply when marking to market isn't possible, because reference exchange prices for an asset in a liquid market are unavailable. In these situations, fair value is assigned using model-derived calculations, based on specified financial assumptions.

Other-than-temporary impairment. The process of marking down the value of financial assets under HCA, to reflect nontemporary losses in value associated with realized credit risk (i.e., default).

Procyclicality. In finance, a situation in which mutually reinforcing behaviors produce a positive feedback loop, resulting in spiraling instability and contagion.

Prudential regulation. Government oversight of deposit-taking institutions to limit their risk-taking and ensure adequate capital and stability.

Systemic risk. (1) Contagion of financial risk across institutions, in a manner that is self-perpetuating and threatens the stability of the system as a whole; (2) risk of disruption to the entire financial system, or to one or more core functions within it.

Summary

Fair value accounting (FVA) refers to the practice of periodically revaluing an asset, ideally by reference to current prices in a liquid market. FVA is commonly distinguished from the competing method of *historical cost accounting* (HCA), in which the book value of an asset is based on the price that was originally paid for it. In the wake of the 2008 financial crisis, controversy erupted over whether FVA was a major driver of the crisis, allegedly forcing banks and financial institutions to write down the value of assets on their books in a self-perpetuating spiral of devaluation, panic selling, and loss of liquidity. That controversy amplified a much longer-running historical debate about whether FVA or HCA is the better approach to valuing financial assets, and which approach provides the most useful information to key stakeholder groups, including investors and prudential regulators. Particularly for policymakers concerned with the stability of financial institutions and of the financial system as whole, these sorts of debates obscure a more basic set of questions concerning the connections between FVA, HCA, and systemic risk and related avenues for making both the financial system and its underlying accounting information more robust.

Study Purpose and Methods

The purpose of this study was broadly to investigate FVA and HCA policy issues and evidence in the wake of the financial crisis, and to explore and explain the relevance of the accounting standards and the recent debate to a nontechnical policy audience. More specifically, we sought to address two basic questions in some depth:

1. What is the relationship between accounting standards (FVA and HCA) and "systemic risk" (i.e., the contagion of financial risk across institutions, with the potential to destabilize the entire financial system)?
2. What kinds of regulatory, governance, and accounting standards options might policymakers consider to respond to related concerns about systemic risk?

To address these questions, we conducted an extensive review of published literature and a series of interviews with a range of stakeholders and experts concerning various facets of FVA, HCA, risk management, risk regulation, and the financial services industry.

Key Findings

Based on our review, we found the following:

1. Both FVA and HCA can be associated with systemic risk to the financial system under some circumstances.
2. Available empirical evidence does not provide strong support for the claim that FVA was a primary driver of the 2008 financial crisis.
3. When implemented poorly, both FVA and HCA can produce misleading information and lead to risk accumulation problems and the potential for market distortion.
4. Improving the quality of both FVA and HCA information in financial statements should be a priority consideration for policymakers.

Avenues for pursuing such improvement could include augmenting current disclosure requirements connected with both FVA and HCA, strengthening valuation processes and management controls within financial firms, and reinforcing the strength of independent audit and regulatory oversight with regard to those processes. Each of these findings is explored in more detail below.

FVA and Systemic Risk

Could FVA pose a systemic risk to the financial sector? Some theoretical accounts (which also underpin FVA's presumed role in spreading risk in the 2008 crisis) point to FVA as a vector for spreading risk-contagion across the financial sector. The basic premise, in theory, is that an initial economic shock could force one institution to sell some of its assets, thereby exposing it to short-run market illiquidity and forcing it to accept a lower price than the assets' fundamental value. When FVA standards apply, other banks that hold similar assets would then be forced to make changes to their own books to reflect the lower price obtained by the first institution. That could then place the other banks under financial pressure and force them to sell assets into the illiquid market to fulfill their own regulatory capital constraints. The theoretical result is the spread of risk across otherwise independent institutions, contributing to an accelerating spiral of devaluation that could culminate in a wave of institutional insolvencies.

The logic behind this view of FVA-induced contagion has been formalized in economic liquidity pricing models, which suggest that this scenario could indeed happen given specific starting assumptions. This being said, some of the key starting assumptions (relating to FVA and regulatory capital constraints) are arguably rigid and not congruent with real-world conditions in 2008, nor do the models appear to provide a simple explanation of the causes or the unfolding of the 2008 economic crisis. Indeed, we reviewed all of the post-2008 empirical studies of the relationship between FVA and the crisis through quantitative data on banks, their assets, their stock values, etc. Based on our reading of the six key studies addressing this point, we conclude that the empirical evidence available to date does not provide compelling support that FVA was the primary driver of the crisis, or of associated bank insolvencies, in 2008.

HCA and Systemic Risk

While recent controversy has focused more on the link between FVA and systemic risk, HCA can also be associated with systemic risk. In particular, when HCA is erroneously applied to assets without accurate adjustment for permanent reduction in value (known as impairment), the result can be to accumulate and conceal asset risks in a firm's financial statements. And when large numbers of firms hold similar assets and similarly account inaccurately for impairment, the resulting problems can easily become systemic. The historical case studies of the savings and loans (S&L) crisis of the 1980s and the less developed country (LDC) crisis of the 1970s illustrate this point: Both cases involved the accumulation of risky assets by financial institutions, under the cloak of a widespread failure to account accurately for other-than-temporary impairment in those assets. In both instances, U.S. policymakers eventually had to intervene to stabilize and recapitalize vulnerable financial institutions.

One of the important takeaway lessons from these events is simply that HCA, too, has been associated with past systemic risk episodes, and that misleading or unfaithful application of HCA principles (particularly with regard to impairment accounting) poses its own forms of risk. A related lesson is that financial institutions sometimes have the incentive to accumulate financial risk, rather than to disclose it, when confronted with the potential for insolvency—a phenomenon that has been aptly described by others as "gambling for resurrection."

Implementation and Governance Issues Pertaining to Asset Valuation
Beyond investigating the generic ways in which valuation approaches can be associated with systemic risk, an additional focal point of our study involved the observation that both FVA and HCA approaches are capable of generating poor-quality information when implemented poorly. Neither FVA nor HCA operates in a vacuum; both approaches depend on support from corporate controls and outside monitoring (such as independent audit and regulatory oversight) in order to achieve good implementation, and thereby to generate good financial information. In turn, effective implementation of FVA and HCA may be important to effective institutional risk management, such that stronger valuation practices and related governance processes may help to safeguard institutions against risk. Both approaches to valuation notably involve their own implicit weaknesses and assumptions. Even when implementation is strong, neither approach is likely to be perfect in the financial information that it generates.

Implementation and governance issues pertaining to FVA and HCA tie back to the problem of systemic risk in several ways. First, systemic risk frequently originates from, or is triggered by, institutional risk. Thus, it follows that weaknesses in FVA and HCA that contribute to institutional risk have the potential to contribute to or exacerbate systemic risk as well. Second, the informational quality of FVA and HCA financial statements is of great importance to prudential and systemic risk regulators,[1] just as it is to investors. When the quality of information contained in financial statements is poor or distorted, then regulators may also be impaired in assessing risk and in responding to it effectively. Finally, a related point is the basic observation that regardless of which valuation approach is used (FVA or HCA), there may be an important distinction to draw between institutions that pursue that approach well versus those that do so poorly or ineffectively. These distinctions in the fidelity of valuation could also sometimes have systemic implications and impact, such as by undercutting market confidence in the meaningfulness of accounting information and thereby contributing to episodes of liquidity pricing.

---

[1]   For purposes of this report, we distinguish between "prudential regulation," which focuses on ensuring the institutional solvency of individual banks, and "systemic risk regulation," which focuses on ensuring the stability of the financial system as a whole. In practice, a single federal agency (e.g., the Federal Reserve) may carry out responsibilities in both of these areas.

Conclusions and Recommendations

We conclude that policymakers concerned with systemic risk in the wake of the 2008 crisis have at times been preoccupied with the wrong set of questions about FVA. In our view, whether FVA caused the 2008 crisis and which of FVA or HCA is the "better" accounting approach are not the most useful questions to focus on. Based on our reading of the available empirical evidence, we conclude that FVA was probably not a primary driver of the 2008 crisis, nor does the history of the crisis comport well with the theory of an FVA-induced, pro-cyclicality spiral of asset sales and markdowns, culminating in widespread bank insolvencies. Meanwhile, the long-running debate over whether FVA or HCA is objectively "better" is also likely a canard for policymakers whose practical concern is strengthening the financial system against systemic risk.

Based on our review, we conclude that both FVA and HCA can produce useful information, that both can be vulnerable to producing misinformation when not applied rigorously, and that both are capable of contributing to systemic risk in some circumstances. In order to generate high-quality financial information, both approaches depend on rigorous implementation, strong support from governance and controls within financial institutions, and on meaningful oversight through independent audit and regulatory processes. When those supports are weak and the quality of accounting information generated is poor, then both of FVA and HCA can contribute to the accumulation of institutional risk and to various channels for contagion and systemic risk across the financial sector.

Given the foregoing, the more important question for policymakers to focus on, with regard to accounting standards and systemic risk, is this:

- How can FVA and HCA, and the financial information that *both* methods generate, be improved to better protect against systemic risk to the banking sector in the future?

In answering the question, it is important to consider what kinds of changes in institutional practice, accounting standards, and prudential oversight might support improved protection against systemic risk. The ultimate challenge is to identify reasonable prospects for reform along these lines, recognizing the implicit trade-off with any increase in costs to the private sector associated with more burdensome accounting or regulatory requirements.

Based on our review and research on these issues, we suggest several related avenues for policymakers to explore, each reflecting a potential direction for reform. We offer these as broad options for policymakers and standard-setters to consider, rather than as formal recommendations. In particular, the costs and benefits associated with any of these options would need to be assessed in detail and would likely depend on fine points of implementation beyond the scope of our current study. Regardless, the options that follow illustrate a range of leverage points that could be tapped in the future, in efforts to strengthen accounting practice and standards under both FVA and HCA while reducing related risks to the financial system.

Governance

- *Policymakers should consider new steps to strengthen institutional governance and control mechanisms that in turn support higher-quality FVA and HCA practices within financial firms.* The fidelity of accounting information is unlikely to exceed the quality of whatever institutional process generates it. Stronger regulatory guidance and oversight protecting the integrity of the valuation process, and of the management and corporate governance framework that supports it, could help to improve the quality of both FVA and HCA information, and thereby safeguard against risk accumulation and contagion among financial firms.

- *Policymakers could strengthen FVA and HCA approaches to valuation by improving audit oversight in connection with both approaches.* To the extent that auditors face significant challenges in providing rigorous oversight for mark-to-model valuations under FVA, and for the evaluation of other-than-temporary impairments under HCA, policymakers ought to consider ways to strengthen and better support auditors in performing that oversight.

Standard Setting

- *Policymakers should consider tightening generally accepted accounting principles (GAAP) standards in connection with both FVA and HCA, to improve the quality of information provided about the impact of liquidity pricing on each valuation approach.* Given that problems with the two approaches tend to arise in the context of liquidity pricing and in accounting for other-than-temporary impairment, it follows that more explicit guidelines for dealing with these problems under the standards might be helpful in producing more consistent financial disclosures.

- *Policymakers should clarify whether financial statements truly are required to disclose sufficient detail about FVA mechanics to allow users of financial statements to reconstruct and assess the details of valuation models for themselves.* Current GAAP standards under ASC 820[2] do seem to require this level of disclosure in connection with mark-to-model valuations and level 3 inputs,[3] but a cursory review of actual fair value disclosures in bank financial statements makes it far less clear what's actually required in practice here.

- *Policymakers should consider developing or adding metrics of valuation robustness to augment standard financial disclosures under GAAP.* One way to build on existing FVA and HCA disclosures in financial statements would be to develop better metrics to rate the quality of valuation processes and the data that flow from them. Existing value-at-risk (VaR) based calculations offer one possible avenue for such metrics, by seeking to quantify the magnitude of observable variation around a point estimate of fair value for an asset portfolio. Complementary metrics might be developed to focus on the quality of the institutional controls and governance that support the valuation process, or on the quality and recency of any reference market prices used in FVA.

- *Policymakers and standard-setters should consider adding disclosure requirements to address situations in which market power and other forms of price endogeneity are likely to influence FVA observed market values.* In particular, when the holder of an asset has concentrated ownership and faces a thin market for selling it, then the holder's own choices about

---

[2]   ASC 820 refers to a May 2011 update of the Financial Accounting Standards Board's Accounting Standards Codification titled "Fair Value Measurement" (FASB, 2011).

[3]   "Level 3 inputs" are unobservable inputs that correspond to assumptions made by a reporting institution, concerning the assumptions that market participants would use in pricing an asset. See discussion in appendix on the hierarchy of inputs to fair value measurement, as specified in GAAP per ASC 820.

whether or not to sell may substantially affect both the supply and market price of the asset.

Prudential Regulation

- *Regulators should consider, when strengthening regulatory capital requirements, the potential for perverse asset valuation and institutional governance effects.* The aim in strengthening institutional capital requirements (as under Basel III[4]) is typically to help make banks stronger and more resilient to shocks. For that aim to be met, however, banks actually need to fulfill the more rigorous requirements. To the extent that asset valuation practices are unreliable, opaque, and/or subject to distortion, then it may be difficult for outsiders to know how well the strengthened requirements are truly being met.

- *Regulators should evaluate whether asset risk-weighting in bank capital requirements has the potential to contribute to perverse risk effects and contagion, in connection with FVA.* One area for concern in systemic oversight is the possibility that risk-weighting of assets might sometimes create an incentive for banks to preferentially liquidate an asset valued with FVA over alternative categories of non-FVA assets, at a time when doing so magnifies the likelihood of procyclicality, erosion in asset value, and spreading weakness to the regulatory capital of other institutions.

- *Prudential regulators should consider playing a more prominent role in vetting asset valuation practice at large institutions.* The prudential regulators are a key stakeholder group in using FVA and HCA information for risk oversight, and they also occupy a unique position in having influence over, and visibility into, multiple financial institutions at the same time. As illustrated by the 2009 Supervisory Capital Assessment Program, regulatory oversight can be used to investigate and help buttress the fidelity of valuation across institutions, while imposing some common baseline assumptions on related practice.

---

[4]   Basel III is a global, voluntary regulatory standard on bank capital adequacy. See Basel Committee on Banking Supervision (2010).

Acknowledgments

We would like to thank our RAND colleagues Susan Gates, Paul Heaton, Lloyd Dixon, and Michael Gallagher for their thoughtful review and suggestions on this manuscript. We are likewise indebted to Professor Franklin Allen for his review and input. Additional thanks are due to Sarah Hauer, Pam Calig, James Torr, and Jocelyn Lofstrom for their help in editing, managing, and supporting the preparation of this document.

We would also like to acknowledge the comments and suggestions offered to us by the RAND Institute for Civil Justice and Center for Corporate Ethics and Governance Boards of Advisors, and particularly those from Robert Jackson, Robert Garrett, Steve Strongin, Chris Pettit, Larry Zicklin, Paul Roth, and the Honorable Arthur Levitt.

Abbreviations

AC	Allen and Carletti
ASC	Accounting Standards Codification
CDO	collateralized debt obligation
DIDMCA	Institutions Deregulation and Monetary Control Act of 1980
FAS	Financial Accounting Standard
FASB	Financial Accounting Standards Board
FDIC	Federal Deposit Insurance Corporation
FHLBB	Federal Home Loan Bank Board
FRBC	Federal Reserve Bank of Chicago
FSP	FASB Staff Position
FVA	fair value accounting
GAAP	Generally Accepted Accounting Principles
HCA	historical cost accounting
IASB	International Accounting Standards Board
IFRS	International Financial Reporting Standards
IMF	International Monetary Fund
LDC	less developed country
S&L	savings and loans
SCAP	Supervisory Capital Assessment Program
SEC	U.S. Securities and Exchange Commission
SFAS	Statement of Financial Accounting Standards
SSG	Senior Supervisors Group

CHAPTER ONE

Introduction

Fair value accounting (FVA) refers to the practice of periodically revaluing an asset (or a liability), based on current prices in a liquid market.[1] Fair value accounting is commonly distinguished from the competing method of *historical cost accounting* (HCA), in which the book value of an asset is based on the price that was originally paid for it. In practice, both of these perspectives on asset valuation are deeply embedded in the generally accepted accounting principles (GAAP) framework in the United States, and each is defined by an elaborate set of accounting standards, methods, and metrics.[2] The details of how FVA and HCA apply to different financial accounting situations can be complex, and difficult to fathom for nonaccountants. The details are nevertheless important, because the accounting standards define the anatomy of the financial disclosures that public companies are required to make as a part of their regular securities filings with the U.S. Securities and Exchange Commission (SEC). Moreover, the accounting standards are also deeply tied to the prudential regulation of financial institutions (including banks) and, by extension, to assessing the adequacy of bank capital reserves. In sum, FVA and HCA are of central importance both to investors and regulators in determining the basic informational substrate for evaluating the financial well-being of public companies and banking institutions.

FVA became a focus for intense scrutiny and debate during the financial crisis of 2008, when some argued that fair value and "mark-to-market" practices[3] had been a primary factor in contributing to the crisis and to the eruption of systemic risk among large financial institutions.[4] The argument was generally that initial downward pressure on the prices of mortgage-backed securities and related assets fed through to institutional balance sheets via FVA, which in turn led to increasing sales of those assets to raise additional capital (particularly among large banks). The sales then allegedly contributed to additional downward momentum in asset prices, further eroding institutional capital, and to subsequent rounds of compulsory selling as banks struggled to meet their regulatory capital requirements and/or fulfill counterparty collateral requirements in the face of the crunch.

---

[1] A "liquid market" is one in which there is an abundance of ready buyers and sellers for an asset, and consequently in which it is easy to determine the market-clearing price for that asset.

[2] Both approaches are also embedded in the accounting framework of the International Financial Reporting Standards (IFRS), which has been adopted by many other parts of the world. See also discussion on IFRS convergence in the appendix to this report.

[3] Mark-to-market is the most basic version of FVA and involves assigning a price to an asset based on the publicly quoted price for the same asset trading on an exchange, ideally in a liquid market.

[4] See, e.g., Gingrich (2008); Forbes (2009); Isaac (2009a).

Arguments and Counterarguments About FVA

Several related arguments were also made by FVA critics. First was that the very notion of an objective "market price" may be fundamentally misleading under conditions of extreme illiquidity. Second was the idea that FVA might contribute to risk contagion among a group of financial institutions with strongly correlated investment portfolios and/or a network of counterparty financial relationships among themselves. Third was that forcing banks to mark to market during a crisis could have the effect of compelling asset sales in response to transient market conditions, when the banks might otherwise have realized a much better price on their assets simply by holding onto them longer. Implicitly, all of these arguments tie back to the valuation alternative of HCA and the premise that HCA would be more robust to these sorts of problems involving distorted market prices and financial risk.

The counterarguments made in favor of FVA are numerous. Advocates of FVA have suggested that fair value actually provides more transparency in balance sheets rather than less, and that rigorous FVA practice makes speculative bubbles less likely to accumulate in the first place.[5] It has also been pointed out, of course, that the crisis involved a complex tapestry of events and antecedent conditions, including widespread opportunism and deception in the origination of home mortgages; securitization of mortgages into a hierarchy of exotic pooled investments with poorly understood risk characteristics; and over-leveraging of the finance pipeline for residential real estate at multiple points within the system.[6] Whether FVA is best understood as a primary causal factor in the crisis, or as a minor accelerant in an episode of financial deleveraging that would have occurred anyway, remains a point of heated debate. Among the financial institutions that actually failed during the crisis, it has been observed that some primarily held trading securities and other assets subject to FVA treatment, while others focused their business on hold-to-maturity assets that received HCA treatment. Concentrated exposure to FVA in the balance sheet was neither a necessary nor sufficient condition for the banks that went insolvent during the crisis.[7] In turn, this suggests that the role of FVA in the crisis may be more nuanced than any simple explanation might imply.

Both the recent financial crisis and the long-running historical debate over which of FVA or HCA is "better" invite some basic threshold reflection on the two accounting approaches, and how they work in practice. For example, to what degree do FVA and HCA differ in their underlying mechanics, and in the ways that they incorporate different aspects of risk (e.g., credit and liquidity) into the process of establishing asset values? Are embedded assumptions about the quality of accounting information, and of auditing, important to understand in reading financial statements, regardless of whether FVA or HCA is used to prepare them? And is there a basic alignment between FVA and HCA standards and different business models, such that it makes particular sense to use FVA in some contexts and HCA in others? We explore these threshold issues in some detail in Chapter Two, as well as in the appendix to this report.

---

[5]   See, e.g., CFA Institute (2010).

[6]   See discussion in Financial Crisis Inquiry Commission (2011).

[7]   See discussion in Chapter Four. See also SEC (2008).

Systemic Risk, Accounting Standards, and Prudential Regulation

For our purposes in this report, the most important questions about FVA and HCA involve their relationship to "systemic risk"—i.e., the contagion of financial risk across institutions, with the potential to destabilize an entire financial system or market, as opposed to the simple risk of insolvency for any single financial institution or bank within the system. The crisis of 2008 is notably an example of a "systemic event," in which the insolvency of particular banks and institutions was symptomatic of the dissolution of a broader speculative bubble, and in which some individual bank failures threatened to spread contagion (that is, the risk of insolvency and institutional failures) more broadly.

Questions about systemic risk in the financial system also connect to the regulation of banks[8] and to the relationship between that regulation and accounting standards. Under Federal Reserve rules and in conformance with internationally agreed-upon standards, depository banks are required to maintain a defined fraction of their capital as equity in liquid assets, to ensure their solvency and the ability to pay off liabilities in the ordinary course of business. Regulatory capital requirements for banks tie directly to systemic risk, in that those requirements determine the financial "cushion" that banks have against sudden liquidity shocks and runs on assets—loosely speaking, less cushion means more vulnerability. But it turns out that bank capital requirements are also tied closely to FVA and HCA standards, since the latter play directly into calculations about how much capital banks actually have on hand. One implication, therefore, is that any consideration of the systemic implications of FVA and HCA is likely also to touch on the regulation of banks and of their capital requirements. Another is that accounting standard setting and bank regulation involve complementary areas of policy that intertwine with each other. By extension, modifying one set of standards or rules may have collateral effects on the other, in ways that deserve careful scrutiny by policymakers.

The recent policy debate over the impact and appropriate breadth of FVA standards has historical antecedents that long precede the most recent episode of financial crisis. Related accounting issues were prominent in the savings-and-loan (S&L) crisis of the 1980s, and were also salient during the less developed country (LDC) crisis of the 1970s. Competing views about the relative merits of FVA and HCA approaches led to oscillating accounting practices and standards throughout much of the 20th century. In the 1920s, for example, FVA rather than HCA was more typically the norm in corporate bookkeeping.[9] The history of these accounting issues (and episodes of crisis) provides important context for the long-running dispute about which approach is objectively more accurate and illuminating, particularly with regard to the asset books of banks and other financial institutions. Recent arguments about the merits of expanding FVA treatment to new categories of assets, such as banks' portfolios of loans, have to be viewed in this context. As we will endeavor to show, many of the concerns that have been raised in the recent debate over FVA are only peripherally connected to systemic risk issues.

---

8   Known in finance as "prudential regulation"—that is, regulations intended to protect investors by setting limits on the risks financial institutions may take.

9   See Shearer (2010); SEC (2008).

Purpose of This Study

The current research study was undertaken by the RAND Corporation during late 2010 to early 2012, with support from the Goldman Sachs Global Markets Institute. The aim of the study was to investigate FVA and HCA policy issues in the wake of the financial crisis of 2008, and to explain the relevance of the accounting standards and recent debate to a nontechnical policy audience. We particularly seek to address two basic questions:

1. What is the relationship between accounting approaches (FVA and HCA) and systemic risk?
2. What kinds of regulatory, governance, and accounting standards options might policy-makers consider to respond to concerns about systemic risk?

Although we also touch on a range of other FVA and HCA issues throughout this report, our primary intent is to provide a foundation for understanding the accounting approaches and the recent debate over them, as a platform for addressing these basic questions about systemic risk.

Research Methods

To address these questions, we conducted an extensive review of published literature on FVA, HCA, systemic and institutional risk, and the prudential regulation of banks. The review included both research and academic studies published on these topics, as well as a broad range of regulatory materials and guidance documents, accounting standards and related commentaries and proposals, public opinion letters, reports from various private-sector and nongovernment organizations, and a range of advocacy pieces, articles, and books. We particularly focused on relevant literature published during and after the 2008 financial crisis and on the empirical studies that attempted to examine the influence of FVA in the context of that crisis. We also compiled historical case studies on two major episodes of systemic risk in the financial system: the S&L crisis of the late 1980s and the LDC crisis of the 1970s. We again reviewed a range of published materials and commentaries in putting these case studies together.

Our investigation also drew on extensive interviews with an array of stakeholders and experts concerning various facets of FVA, HCA, risk management, risk regulation, and the financial services industry. In total, we spoke with more than 65 people over the course of the study, including auditors and partners at large accounting firms (3); buy- and sell-side equity and fixed-income analysts (5); current and former government officials (7); current and former representatives from professional accounting organizations and standard-setting groups (6); accounting and finance executives at a range of bank (8) and nonbank financial institutions (15); accounting and finance executives from outside the financial services community (2); officials and executives with accounting organizations and other nonprofit banking and finance organizations (6); and a range of other executives connected with commercial and investment banks (11).

The interviews were conducted either in person or by phone using an open-ended, semi-structured interview protocol. Most of the interviews were conducted between September 2010 and July 2011. Interviews covered the practical application of FVA and HCA in valuing financial assets; the business and risk management implications of FVA and HCA for institutions and regulators; and the link between valuation methods and the prudential oversight of financial institutions. All interviews were conducted on a confidential basis. Notes taken during interviews were subsequently reviewed, coded, and organized by topic area, and then analyzed for recurring themes and distinctive responses across interview participants. We incorporate relevant themes, quotes, and observations from the interviews throughout the body of this report.

In addition to the literature reviews, interviews, and case studies, this research project involved some exploratory analyses of financial and accounting data from banks, drawing particularly on banking data compiled by the Federal Reserve. We undertook these analyses in connection with our review of the literature and of previous empirical studies on FVA and institutional balance sheets, in order to better understand and evaluate the methods and results of those earlier studies.

Organization of This Report

The remainder of this report is organized into chapters corresponding to the major topics explored in this report. Chapter Two provides background on the FVA and HCA approaches and summarizes the long-running debate over the merit of these approaches. Chapters Three and Four focus on systemic risk and accounting standards, and on the prudential regulation of banks, accordingly. Chapter Five reviews two historical episodes involving FVA, HCA, and financial crisis and offers comments on what they teach us about systemic risks issues. Chapter Six explores a series of implementation and governance issues that influence the quality of FVA and HCA information, in ways that can contribute to systemic risk. In the final chapter of this report, we integrate our findings across topic areas and offer a set of conclusions and recommendations on accounting standards and systemic risk for consideration by the policy and business communities.

CHAPTER TWO

Background: The Debate over FVA and HCA

The purpose of standardized accounting is to provide sufficient financial information to investors, shareholders, creditors, managers, and others, so that each can make meaningful assessments about the value and sustainability of firms. In a vacuum, judgments about value can often be subjective. What one person deems to be priceless artwork, for example, might be viewed by another as lacking any merit or value. In the context of the financial world, commonly agreed-upon standards for accounting can help to establish consensus and objectivity in valuation practices. Since financial statements are used by a variety of people for a variety of purposes, commonly agreed-upon accounting standards have been formulated in an effort to provide fair and consistent financial information about firms. In the United States, the basic standards for financial accounting in business are known as generally accepted accounting principles (GAAP).

GAAP includes standards that define both FVA and HCA practice. These standards determine when and how each valuation approach is to be used in the preparation of formal financial statements. In the appendix to this document, we offer a quick overview of the GAAP framework that specifies each of FVA and HCA. We also briefly describe the related modifications to GAAP standards that were enacted around the time of the 2008 financial crisis.

What Are the Sources of Deep Disagreement over FVA and HCA?

Notwithstanding the defining GAAP standards for applying FVA and HCA, there remains a rancorous debate over the merits of these competing approaches, their potential impact on investors and institutions, and their connections to systemic risk. Among accounting experts, regulators, and banking and financial services executives, people's feelings about FVA seem to be deeply divided and passionately held, in ways not fully summarized by or determined based purely on their membership in one or more of these groups.[1] Strong differences of opinion were notably reflected in some of the hearings on FVA organized by the SEC in 2008, and in public comment letters received by the Financial Accounting Standards Board (FASB) in

---

[1] So, for example, many banking institutions and organizations went on record opposing the proposed expansion of fair value standards during 2009 and 2010 (see, e.g., Financial Services Roundtable, 2010). But some significant financial institutions, most notably Goldman Sachs, have been strong advocates for FVA (see, e.g., Goldman Sachs, 2010a, 2010b). Likewise, the U.S. prudential regulators (Federal Reserve, Federal Deposit Insurance Corporation [FDIC], Office of the Comptroller of the Currency [OCC], etc.) were unified in their opposition to expanded fair value treatment (Federal Reserve et al., 2010); but several SEC officials have expressed much more favorable and supportive sentiments about FVA in recent years.

2009, responding to [then] proposed revisions to the FVA standards. We heard similarly strong sentiments about FVA and HCA expressed in our interviews, by partisans on both sides of the FVA spectrum.

Although the debate over FVA grew louder in the wake of the 2008 financial crisis, the debate actually has historical origins that long predate the current episode of financial turmoil.[2] In fact, the current framework of accounting standards and bank regulation that has emerged through recent decades is in part a reflection of a much longer-running debate over the wisdom of FVA versus HCA. For persons previously unfamiliar with the accounting standards and their history, the questions invited by the long-running debate are: Why have people been engaged in a decades-long argument over something so esoteric? What are some of the major underlying differences of opinion and assumption that have contributed to the debate? In turn, how do those key points of disagreement tie back to the relationship of the accounting standards to systemic risk?

What Do Consumers of Accounting Information Really Want to Know?

FVA and HCA, as applied to assets, focus on different basic snapshots of valuation. Each is subject to different problems and limitations. FVA, by definition, involves establishing the current value of an asset, or the price at which the asset could be sold for today, based (whenever possible) on observable market prices. FVA is maximally relevant with regard to assets that are likely to be sold in the near term, and in connection with portfolios of securities that trade on liquid markets, when the clearing prices for the assets are easy to observe and to document. FVA becomes far more complex, and less easily verifiable, as applied to illiquid or non-market-traded securities, when valuations are based on finance models rather than markets, and when the assumptions that go into generating an FVA "price" may be obscure or of questionable validity. FVA may also be less relevant as a valuation method when applied to an asset that the owner has no intention of selling in the near future.

By contrast, HCA involves valuing an asset based on a historical price, defined by what the owner of the asset originally paid to acquire it. HCA is backward looking, and it does not involve adjusting the book value of an asset to reflect transient volatility or fluctuations in the market, nor for unrealized appreciation over time. HCA valuations are, however, supposed to be adjusted to reflect other-than-temporary impairments to the value of an asset, as when credit defaults in a portfolio of mortgages degrade the future flow of revenue that will be realized from those mortgages.[3] Because of the nature of HCA valuation, the approach enjoys the advantages of being less volatile, less responsive to liquidity shock, less vulnerable to speculative run-up in asset prices, and less assumption-dependent than is sometimes the case for FVA valuation. For these reasons, HCA may provide particularly useful information in pricing the assets of a "going-concern" business, in which the intent is to hold the assets for a long period of time, and in which there is no likelihood of an insolvency that would compel a sale of the assets. HCA valuations may become misleading, however, when these assumptions are vio-

---

[2]   See, e.g., discussion in Cascini and DelFavero (2011).

[3]   In the context of a market characterized by significant credit risk and rising default rates, the adjustment of HCA asset values to reflect instances of other-than-temporary impairment becomes highly consequential. This was surely the case in 2008, and debate continues in the wake of the collapse over whether mortgage assets on banks' books, traditionally dealt with under HCA, have been appropriately adjusted for impairment. See, e.g., Rapoport (2011).

lated, or when the impairment of assets to reflect nontemporary credit problems has been inaccurate or misleading.

A central underlying point of dispute in arguments about FVA is whether one or the other of these approaches provides "better" financial information, and if so, better for whom? Implicitly, investors who have a short time horizon on assets (as often applies to securities held for trading) will tend to be more interested in an FVA approach to understanding the value of the assets. The same is likewise true for investors seeking to assess the financial position of a firm or institution, when the latter faces a serious potential for insolvency.[4] On the other hand, for investors seeking to assess the status of a going-concern business in which there is no risk of bankruptcy, HCA is sometimes viewed as a better index of the fundamental, long-run value of the assets of the firm: particularly so when the firm has no intention of selling or trading the assets in question, and when liquidity effects distort short-run prices in trading markets. In other words, different kinds of investors may have different perspectives about whether FVA or HCA is more useful or appropriate, depending both on the assets and the firms involved and on the investment context in which the financial information is going to be used. Both accounting approaches may offer useful (and nonduplicative) information in some circumstances.[5]

Do Different Types of Users of Accounting Information Want to Know Different Things?

Another implicit point of disagreement centers on for whom the accounting information is actually being generated, and the primary purposes for which the information is going to be used. In practice, there clearly can be lots of different users of accounting information, including banks and financial services firms themselves (in tracking their own status and managing portfolio risk), contractual counterparties (in assessing the solvency of their partners in financial transactions), and equity analysts and economists (in assessing the financial status and risk of particular companies, market sectors, etc.), to name just a few. But in principle, two of the most important categories of users arguably overshadow most of the other groups and potentially have somewhat different perspectives and needs in how they use accounting information, and consequently different views about FVA and HCA. Those categories are investors (and particularly, investors in public company securities and stock) and regulators, respectively.

Investors

The investor community relies on accounting statements and financial information. The securities law framework in the United States requires standardized financial disclosures on the part of public companies, intended to protect and empower investors by serving their informational needs. Meanwhile, both the accounting standards promulgated by FASB and the

---

[4]   Even in these instances, though, investors' interest in FVA assessments of asset value may be tempered by whether an asset is being valued by market or by model and, in the latter case, by the transparency, clarity, and validity of the assumptions in the model.

[5]   As we discuss next, different users of accounting information are on record as favoring either FVA or HCA as being more appropriate or illuminating for their own purposes. We encountered similar diversity of views in our own interviews with stakeholders. This raises another question, however. Do all users of accounting information share the same underlying interest in assessing the current prospects and financial situation of institutions? Or do they differ, even in this regard? The answer to this question is subtle, and in part ties to a discussion of varying time horizons for investment, which may lead some investors to be far more interested in FVA information than others. We will return to the topic of investment time horizons later in Chapter Two and in Chapter Six.

SEC regulatory requirements that build on those standards are aimed in large part at investor protection. Given that public company investors are some of the primary intended recipients of accounting information, one question that follows is, Is there reason to believe that those investors (as a group) are better served by an FVA or HCA approach to the assets on firms' balance sheets? The answer is both yes and no: Some investors appear to prefer FVA information, while others prefer HCA. Many accounting experts and investor advocates have argued that an FVA approach provides more transparency in firms' financial statements, and therefore is generally more consistent with promoting investor welfare. Others, however, have disputed those arguments, particularly by challenging whether FVA, as applied to nonliquid, nontrading assets, really does provide much incremental transparency.[6]

Regulators

The regulatory community comprises a second key group of consumers of accounting information. Several U.S bank regulatory agencies, including the Federal Reserve, the Federal Deposit Insurance Corporation (FDIC), and the Office of the Comptroller of the Currency (OCC), rely on accounting information (and on the accounting standards) as a basic resource in overseeing the status and solvency of banks and other financial institutions. The institutional role of these prudential agencies is very different from that of investor protection (which is the focus of the SEC): Their focus is instead on safeguarding the solvency of banking institutions, the interests of depositors, and/or protecting the stability of the banking system as a whole. Prudential regulators, too, make use of accounting information about financial services firms, as an important resource in helping to ensure institutional solvency and monitoring risk. These regulators, however, have not been advocates for expanding the application of FVA to new categories of assets on bank balance sheets. In fact, the agencies collectively have tended to oppose increased application of FVA principles: In particular, they issued an opinion letter opposing FASB's 2009 FVA proposal to this end.[7] In their opinion letter, the prudential agencies asserted that for purposes of banking oversight, the volatility associated with FVA could be highly problematic, and by implication, that HCA standards provide more useful and more stable information for their purposes.[8]

To the extent that different types of users of accounting information have fundamentally different informational needs and agendas to pursue, those differences surely contribute to subsequent disputes about the relative merits of, and appropriate contours for, FVA and HCA. Here again, the point is not that one side or the other of the debate is clearly superior. Rather, given multiple types of users with varying needs for, and perspectives on, accounting information, it's possible for partisans of both FVA and HCA to have valid information preferences,

---

[6]   Compare, e.g., CFA Institute (2009) (arguing on behalf of the usefulness of expanded FVA disclosures from the perspective of investors) and Smith (2010) (summarizing investor arguments and comments received by FASB that disputed the usefulness of expanding FVA disclosures). In the context of our own interviews, one bank equity analyst notably commented that it was easier for him to use HCA information in financial statements because he felt he knew exactly how that information was derived. By contrast, he felt that FVA information on non-market-traded assets involved many more embedded and opaque assumptions, making it more difficult for him to know how much confidence to put in the numbers. Another analyst observed that it is difficult for an outsider to assess how "good" the FVA process is at a particular institution, when analyzing its financial statements, and that more transparency and disclosure about the process could significantly improve the quality of related financial statements.

[7]   See Federal Reserve et al. (2010).

[8]   Federal Reserve et al. (2010).

despite the fact that those preferences may superficially appear to be in conflict. Put another way, it may well be that both FVA and HCA have important roles to play in structuring financial disclosure and ensuring that needed information is available to different groups of users.

How Are Business Models and Investment Time Frames Relevant?

Both financial firm business models and the time horizon for investment are factors that sometimes divide the partisans of FVA and HCA, and that may be relevant in considering whether an HCA or FVA approach provides more useful information in a given context. With regard to firm business model, consider a financial services firm that operates primarily by trading securities in the open market. Such a firm is engaged in a business that involves lots of short-term buying and selling of assets, under conditions in which objective market prices for the assets are readily available. For a firm that operates in this way, FVA is a tractable and highly relevant approach to summarizing the value of the firm at any given point in time. At the opposite extreme is a financial services firm (say, a commercial bank) that mainly buys and holds long-term assets (as in the origination of bank loans), with the expectation of drawing a future stream of revenue from those assets. When the firm has no intention of selling or trading the assets to take advantage of fluctuations in market price, then an HCA approach to pricing the firm's assets (as a reflection of long-run value) may be better aligned with the firm's business model: again, a business model based not on taking advantage of transient asset prices in the market, but rather on fundamental asset values (i.e., the discounted present value of the future stream of returns associated with each asset). Thus, depending on the business model of any particular financial firm, either FVA or HCA may more naturally align with the kinds of assets the firm holds and the intent of the firm in seeking to make money from those assets.

In a similar vein, the investment time horizon for holding an asset is also conceptually pertinent to determining which accounting approach may convey more useful information. For a firm that holds assets with the intent to buy and sell *quickly*, as soon as the market price hits an advantageous value to liquidate, then FVA clearly offers the relevant answer for what the value of the assets are at any given point in time. But for another firm that holds similar investments, but in which there is no intent to sell the assets at all, then the liquidation value of the assets at any given point in time may not be especially helpful to understanding the long-run value of those assets for that firm.[9] Here again, when assets are going to be held for the long term, and when there is no plan or intent to sell them and no risk of insolvency in the firm that holds them, then an HCA approach that focuses on fundamental asset values may arguably provide more useful information about the financial status of the assets, and of the firm. As more than one interview respondent told us, the time horizon of investment can be highly material in deciding what kind of accounting information and which accounting approach is likely to be more useful in understanding the financial position of a firm.

Although many of the people we spoke to believed that business model and time horizon offer important insights about which accounting approach is more appropriate in particular situations, there are also persons who strongly disagree with that point of view. Some advo-

---

[9]   In suggesting that FVA asset prices may sometimes be out of alignment with the long-run value for the same assets, one implication is that market prices are not always strong-form efficient. In many economics models and theories, strong-form efficiency of markets is a default assumption, and asset prices are assumed to reflect all relevant information. In the context of liquidity pricing, however, the efficient markets assumption is violated, and consequently the market price for assets may deviate from the discounted present value of the future revenue stream associated with the assets.

cates do believe that one accounting approach (either FVA or HCA) is broadly superior to the other. Strong critics of FVA have suggested that associated risks of procyclicality are so great that FVA is fundamentally problematic and misleading as applied to important categories of bank assets. At the opposite extreme, strong advocates of FVA have sometimes argued that it is fundamentally the more accurate and immediate reflection of asset values, no matter what assets are involved, and regardless of the intended time horizon of a firm's business model or investments. Current standards under GAAP notably align with a mixed approach to this debate over FVA and HCA: namely, in specifying that a mixture of FVA and HCA approaches are appropriate in different instances, and that neither approach is uniformly superior to the other in the information that it provides.

Asset Volatility: Error or Information?
Another serious point of disagreement between partisans of FVA and HCA often involves their perspectives on volatility in asset prices, and their views on whether or not such volatility itself provides useful information for understanding asset (and firm) values. Because FVA involves periodically updating asset values based on current prices in liquid markets,[10] fair values for assets will fluctuate with the market on a periodic (perhaps quarterly, perhaps daily) basis. For some kinds of assets, such as trading securities, those fluctuations may be highly consequential and meaningful. In particular, trading of securities is a business in which daily entry and exit from particular positions is the basis for generating revenue, and daily prices are the metric for deciding whether to buy or sell assets. For firms that operate in this way, and for assets that are typically traded, volatility in prices is a basic part of the information that is needed to understand the financial position of a firm at any given point in time. Put another way, FVA provides a window on the most up-to-date and accurate values that are available concerning these sorts of assets, and the firms that own them, at any designated point of observation.

Opponents and critics of FVA, particularly as the latter applies to banks and to some important categories of bank assets, have a very different perspective on volatility. Critics of FVA sometimes argue that volatility in spot prices for assets, and particularly for assets that the banks have no intention of selling, is fundamentally misleading as an indicator of asset values in the hands of those banks. Here again, the argument is made that where the expressed intent of the bank is to hold a long-term asset in order to realize a stream of future income (as with a mortgage loan), then market prices based on liquidating the asset may be irrelevant or misleading as applied to valuation on the bank's balance sheet.[11] Moreover, it is also sometimes argued that volatility in asset values itself causes problems for bank management and oversight, either because volatility makes it very difficult to maintain stable reserves to meet regulatory capital requirements (discussed further in Chapter Four), or because the simple calculation of asset values becomes highly burdensome or expensive for banks to do on a frequent basis, particularly for large portfolios of non-exchange-traded assets (such as mortgages or commercial loans). The former argument is notably a position espoused by some current and former bank

---

[10]   Or alternately based on financial models, where market prices for assets are unavailable.

[11]   The argument becomes stronger with the added proviso of asset markets in which liquidity pricing and less-than-perfect information apply. In other words, from the perspective of bank investors, to the extent that a bank is well-capitalized and doesn't need to sell its hold-to-maturity assets, then day-to-day fluctuations in the value of the assets become far less relevant. It's only when a forced liquidation of assets is threatened that spot market prices abruptly become the relevant metric for understanding the value of assets that would otherwise be viewed as hold-to-maturity investments.

regulators, while the latter was an argument made by several of the banking executives and advocates with whom we spoke.[12]

The question about whether FVA-induced volatility is fundamentally important, and a reflection of value in its own right, or instead a nuisance in financial measurement that may be costly to track but is largely immaterial, ties back to several of the points already raised above. Who is the prospective user of the accounting information? What do they plan to use the information for? What is the business model of the firm that is holding the asset, and what is the time horizon of the investment at issue? Stakeholders with different answers to these basic questions tend to have very different perspectives on volatility, and on the relative merits of FVA and HCA. And often those stakeholders find themselves in disagreement about which accounting approach is "better," and about the appropriate contours for applying FVA and HCA.

Is Either Accounting Approach More Subject to Misinformation?

Still another point over which partisans of FVA and HCA tend to disagree is the extent to which one or the other of the accounting approaches is more vulnerable to generating bad information, or more subject to distortion through bad accounting practice. Criticisms of FVA along these lines were widespread during the financial crisis in 2008, when the liquidity crunch caused some trading markets to dry up, and assets that were ordinarily capable of being priced through objective market quotes suddenly appeared not to be. At the time, disagreements raged about whether alleged "liquidity prices" for assets were in fact "real," and if not, what the appropriate alternative was for pricing the assets under those conditions. Although FASB issued emergency guidance on this point during 2008, intended to offer banks and other institutions more flexibility in applying FVA principles at the height of the crisis, that guidance was also roundly criticized for being inadequate and ambiguous.[13]

Even apart from the application of FVA during an acute crisis, other critics have questioned the robustness of FVA prices as applied to assets not typically traded on liquid markets, in which pricing is done by model, and with model assumptions that may be questionable or less than transparent. As one interview respondent told us, "It is entirely possible for two firms in good faith to value a nontrading asset under two different fair value models, and to book substantially different prices for the asset, both of which are nevertheless valid under GAAP." Another respondent said, "Auditing firms are often not particularly strong in evaluating the models used in determining fair value for illiquid assets. Often, those models are much better understood by the firms and banks that apply them than by the auditors who oversee them."

---

[12] The argument that FVA may be difficult or costly to implement, as applied to the loan book of a traditional commercial bank, basically sidesteps the more fundamental question of whether FVA produces useful information. Presumably, the cost of generating FVA information escalates for loan assets that are nonfungible and not exchange traded; for which considerable judgment and/or sophisticated modeling will be required to generate FVA prices; and for relatively small institutions that hold large quantities of hold-to-maturity loans. We are unable to offer an opinion about how cost-prohibitive FVA truly would be to implement in such instances: We heard conflicting views about this from different stakeholders whom we interviewed.

[13] See particularly Financial Accounting Standard (FAS) 157-4 (FASB, 2009d) and proposed FASB Staff Position (FSP) FAS 157-e (FASB, 2009b) and associated comment letter summary (FASB, 2009c). Both critics and supporters of the FASB guidance noted that it didn't really change the basic FVA framework, and simply emphasized that institutional judgment is required in determining when acute illiquidity makes market prices an inappropriate yardstick for marking the value of assets. See also, e.g., discussion in Johnson and Leone (2009). Note that the current GAAP standard on fair value accounting is codified at ASC 820, "Fair Value Measurement" (FASB, no date-a).

The argument is that FVA prices coming out of these models may sometimes be misleading, opaque, and based on questionable assumptions.[14] The argument is also made that FVA-based valuation models may sometimes be vulnerable to manipulation by firms, and particularly so where the consequences of asset valuation may have very high stakes for the continued solvency of a firm.[15]

Equally serious criticisms have sometimes been leveled against the HCA approach. Notably, HCA prices under GAAP are supposed to be modified to reflect accounting for nontemporary impairments in asset values, as where credit default on a bank loan means that the bank will not be able to realize the full stream of payments to which it would otherwise have been entitled. In practice, the standards governing HCA impairment are complicated, and they were also placed under review by FASB in the wake of the 2008 financial crisis.[16] Several experts we interviewed, however, suggested that impairment accounting in practice involves considerable judgment on the part of banks (and other institutions), that banks are often overly reluctant when it comes to writing other-than-temporary impairments onto their books, and that bank examiners who are called upon to review the books of insolvent institutions often find serious deficiencies in accounting for nontemporary impairments by banks. Put in other words, HCA can be vulnerable to some of the same problems and distortions as FVA when it comes to accounting for other-than-temporary impairment: namely, opacity of practice, subjective judgment, unreasonable optimism, and potential for manipulation.

As we discuss in more detail in Chapter Five, inadequate accounting for impairments contributed significantly to the S&L crisis of the 1980s. More recently, some critics argued that inflated values of assets on bank balance sheets may have contributed to the run-up of the 2008 real estate bubble, and even that U.S. banks still may be carrying large quantities of toxic assets on their balance sheets, without having marked them down to reflect other-than-temporary impairment. In these kinds of instances, the hope is always that the prices for the assets will eventually return to levels close to the historical cost. As some commentators have observed, where HCA valuations are not appropriately modified for impairment, they may sometimes contribute to "gambling for resurrection," that is, the practice of holding on to bad assets to avoid insolvency, by concealing loss of value in hopes of a future rebound in asset prices. In our interviews, we heard radically different viewpoints from several of our respondents about whether the failure to account for other-than-temporary impairment in toxic loan assets remains a major problem in bank balance sheets today.[17]

---

[14]   Of course, these are criticisms that presumably could also be addressed through improved disclosures by institutions regarding their underlying models, methods, and assumptions in generating FVA asset prices.

[15]   So for example, one person we spoke to described increasing discrepancies between reported values in the collateralized debt obligation (CDO) portfolios of several institutions, versus the actual trading prices of the comparative benchmark indices, in 2008. The extent to which any of the discrepancies reflected deliberate manipulation of values, as opposed to sloppy practice or overly optimistic model assumptions, likely varied from institution to institution.

[16]   See then Statement of Financial Accounting Standards (SFAS) 114 (*Accounting by Creditors for Impairment of a Loan* FASB, 2008); see also Proposed FASB Staff Position No. FAS 115-a, FAS 124-a, and EITF 99-20-b (*Recognition and Presentation of Other-Than-Temporary Impairments*) (FASB, 2009a). Note that the corresponding GAAP standards are currently codified in scattered sections of ASC 320, "Investments—Debt and Equity Securities"; ASC 325, "Investments—Other"; and ASC 310, "Receivables" (FASB, no date-a).

[17]   The difference in views was illustrated in the comments of two people we spoke to. One asserted that CDO values broadly fell by 60 percent or more at the height of the financial crisis but had mostly recovered back to par value in the years since, suggesting that underlying assets had never been impaired to anywhere near the degree that the markets initially

Concluding Observations

Many of the traditional arguments about the merits of FVA and HCA involve advocates and stakeholders who appear to be arguing past each other rather than with each other. In other words, different stakeholders often start from very different assumptions in reaching their own views about the competing merits of FVA and HCA. Even the answers to basic questions about who the key consumers of accounting information are and for what purposes accounting information is going to be used can lead respondents to very different conclusions about FVA and HCA and about the evolving contours of accounting policy. On the bright side, one implication is that there may be greater commonality of opinion across the two sides of the debate than is typically recognized. In our interviews, we spoke with partisans on both sides who nevertheless acknowledged that "the other accounting approach can be appropriate in some circumstances" and that both accounting approaches can generate problems when misused, abused, or misapplied.

For purposes of this report, the debate over FVA and HCA elicits two key questions: How do the background differences in assumptions and perspectives on FVA and HCA pertain to the link between accounting standards and systemic risk? Does one or the other approach contribute a greater vulnerability to systemic risk, by virtue of any of the attributes sketched out here? In the next two chapters, we examine in detail the relationship between systemic risk, FVA and HCA accounting standards, and the prudential regulation of banks.

---

suggested. Another person pointed out that there may still be large quantities of overvalued loan assets still held on banks' books without impairment, even years later, based on the hope that the losses in value will eventually prove to be transient.

CHAPTER THREE

Systemic Risk and Accounting Approaches

A central question raised in the wake of the financial crisis of 2008 has been whether accounting standards, and FVA in particular, contributed directly to systemic risk across the entire financial infrastructure. Many critics have argued that the requirement that banks mark their assets to market had the effect during the 2008 crisis of spreading and accelerating a sell-off, with the consequence of further eroding asset prices and creating a feedback loop of deleveraging, evaporating liquidity, and destabilized bank balance sheets and income statements.

Several of our interviewees related a version of this story. Yet this perspective raises several questions. What is "systemic risk" in this context? What is the implication of suggesting that FVA *causes*, or *contributes to*, systemic risk? In context, is it sufficient that a single systemically important entity (like a Citigroup or an AIG) finds itself in difficulty by virtue of mark-to-market requirements, and that the risk to that entity is then transferred to other institutions by contractual commitments? Or is something stronger and qualitatively different implied when we suggest that FVA itself contributes to "systemic" risk? Given that the 2008 crisis was systemically important, it seems almost tautological to say that the use of FVA during that crisis was in some way associated with systemic impact. To understand the role of FVA in the 2008 crisis, and more broadly its relationship to systemic risk, the key question becomes: How important are accounting approaches as a *pathway* for transmitting risk across institutions, and does FVA in particular contribute to the contagion of risk in some unique or special way?

In this chapter, we explore the relationship between accounting standards and episodes of financial crisis and systemic risk. In particular, we focus on how accounting standards *could*, under conditions that might otherwise be considered a "perfect storm," play a role in spreading risk from sectors of the economy and firms that experience direct losses (as when a focused economic shock occurs) to other sectors and firms that would not otherwise be affected but for the transmission by FVA of eroding asset prices. We also consider how this theoretical possibility is incorporated into some liquidity pricing models in economics, and the limits of those models in establishing the magnitude of risk posed by FVA accounting approaches in the real world.

What Is Systemic Risk?

First, it is helpful to pin down what we mean by "systemic risk." The recent academic and trade literature includes a large number of papers dealing with the topic of systemic risk and the recent financial crisis (see Hellwig, 2009, and references therein). At present, the term "systemic risk" has not generated strong consensus around a single formal definition in the economics literature. At its broadest, the term is simply a catchall phrase for referring to any risk shared by, or affecting, the entire financial system, as opposed to risk that pertains more narrowly to particular firms, asset categories, or transactions within the system. Schwarcz, in a 2008 review article, cites several different definitions for the expression "systemic risk":

- The probability that cumulative losses will occur from an event that ignites a series of successive losses along a chain of [financial] institutions or markets comprising . . . a system.
- The potential for a modest economic shock to induce substantial volatility in asset prices, significant reductions in corporate liquidity, potential bankruptcies, and efficiency losses.
- The risk that a default by one market participant will have repercussions on other participants due to the interlocking nature of financial markets.

The common feature of these various definitions is that a trigger event leads to a cascade of instability affecting other financial institutions and/or markets. The trigger event could be an economic shock or institutional failure in one sector of the economy.[1]

For purposes of our discussion of FVA, we focus on a more narrow definition of systemic risk, corresponding to a particular flavor of what economists call "contagion." Contagion involves the transfer of financial instability between institutions or market sectors. For purposes of this report, we focus particularly on instances of contagion between firms or sectors seemingly *without* direct economic connection, such that an initial shock occurring in one sector or firm then spreads to other seemingly independent sectors or firms.[2] In our usage here, "contagion" is distinct from the notion of counterparty risk, which suggests instead that risk is passed directly between two entities that share a contractual or economic relationship with each other.[3] According both to popular anecdote and to theories of liquidity pricing, FVA, but not HCA, is potentially associated with this kind of risk contagion under some specifiable circumstances. We explore the particulars below.

As we will revisit later in this chapter, we do not intend to suggest that contagion is the only form of systemic risk, or the only vector for systemic risk transmission. Rather, contagion offers the most coherent and rigorous definition for exploring a *causal* link between FVA and the possible transmission of risk throughout the financial system.

---

[1]   To the best of our knowledge, the term "systemic risk" was first used in an economics/finance paper in 1994, in a review of a book written by a World Bank economist. See Schwarcz (2008). The term does not originate within economics, finance, or accounting, and, again, it seems to mean different things to different people. In this chapter, we primarily use the term to describe system-wide effects that involve contagion of risk between otherwise unrelated sectors of the economy.

[2]   See, e.g., recent discussion of financial contagion in CNN, "A Greek tragedy: How the Debt Crisis Spread Like a Virus in 'Contagion,'" September 19, 2011. Note that the word "contagion" is also sometimes used far more broadly in the popular press than we intend here. For example, many commentators have recently asserted the threat of a Greek default on sovereign debt puts the rest of the European Union at risk, and particularly that it has the potential to "infect" French and German banks. But this is not the definition for "contagion" that we intend here. To the extent that French and German banks themselves hold Greek debt, then the French and German institutions are directly exposed to related risk, and the French and German economies would therefore be at risk in the event of a Greek default.

[3]   Note that the academic economics literature defines "contagion" more generally as the transmission of shock and instability from one financial institution to others in the system. Such transmission can occur through the interbank market or the payment system (e.g., Allen and Gale, 2000; Freixas, Pargi, and Rochet, 2000), or through information spillovers (e.g., Allen, Babus, and Carletti, 2012), as well as through asset prices. Although we focus on the latter form of risk contagion in this report, it is worth recognizing that FVA and HCA information may feed into other channels for risk transmission as well, and particularly so to the extent that poor valuation practice contributes to episodes of market illiquidity.

Liquidity Pricing and Economic Models of Contagion

One of the most important theoretical contributions to the debate on FVA and systemic risk involves liquidity pricing models in economics. Such models attempt to describe how financial risk might propagate across independent economic sectors and firms, based purely on the occurrence of an isolated liquidity shock[4] and on the subsequent application of accounting standards to asset values.

A common feature of these models is the notion of "liquidity pricing," or asset pricing driven by the availability of capital (i.e., cash) in the trading markets, rather than by the fundamental earning power of the asset (see Diamond and Rajan, 2001 and 2005).[5] Liquidity pricing implies a disparity between the current market-clearing price for an asset versus the discounted stream of future payments that the asset will actually generate. In order for liquidity pricing to obtain, markets must be so illiquid that investors are actually "leaving money on the table": a circumstance that only occurs where there are few liquid investors available in the market who are capable of purchasing assets at their fundamental values.[6] In principle, liquidity pricing can arise in the economy for a variety of different reasons, but all involve a shortage of market participants with sufficient cash and willingness to purchase assets at their fundamental long-term values.[7]

In practice, it can be difficult to identify episodes of liquidity pricing with confidence, based simply on a decline in the observed market price for assets. In any given situation, it is often unclear whether falling asset prices reflect fundamental changes in value (i.e., an erosion in the net present value of the future stream of payments anticipated from an asset) or are instead liquidity-driven.

Our interviews and the popular press notably provide several examples of possible liquidity pricing witnessed during the 2008 financial crisis. For example, in July of 2007, AAA-rated super-senior tranches of collateralized debt obligations (CDOs) fell in value by 30 percent.[8] As Allen and Carletti (2010) noted, if this loss of value in CDOs reflected the true state of the U.S. housing market at the time, then it corresponded to a belief among market participants that, eventually, three-quarters of the subprime securitized mortgages packaged within the CDOs would go into default. One possibility is that investors did indeed have this extreme belief regarding the credit risk embedded in CDOs and the likely prevalence of mortgage defaults. Another possibility is that liquidity pricing drove at least some of the observed loss of value in super-senior tranches of CDOs in July of 2007. At the time, it was impossible to determine

---

[4] By "liquidity shock," we mean an abrupt loss of liquidity, and of ready buyers and sellers for an asset, in a previously fluid asset market.

[5] See also discussion in Allen and Carletti (2010).

[6] Note that "fundamental value" of a financial asset is usually understood to represent the discounted present value of a future stream of payments that the asset would generate. Here again, exactly what that fundamental value is, and what adjustments should be made to reflect probable credit impairments (if any), is open to debate.

[7] For example, liquidity pricing can occur as the result of the interacting institutions with different time horizons for their liabilities, and hence different time horizons on their need for liquidity, such that the price of an asset for some institutions in a crunch may be determined not by the expected future cash flows (i.e., the asset's fundamentals), but rather by the availability of cash in the short-term market. Similar models and explanations are offered by Allen and Carletti (2008); Cifuentes, Ferruccim and Shin (2005); Plantin, Sapra, and Shin (2008); etc.

[8] See discussion in Allen and Carletti (2010).

whether the observed drop in CDO prices was out of line with fundamental credit risks, since no one then knew what the ultimate default rate on mortgages would actually be.

Stipulating that liquidity pricing sometimes does indeed occur in the real world, how does this relate in turn to FVA and risk contagion? A basic idea, often incorporated into models of liquidity pricing, is that the application of FVA to assets may spread liquidity pricing from an initially affected firm or sector of the economy to other independent firms or sectors that would not otherwise be affected.[9] The new firms would then be compelled to write down the prices of assets on their own books, in a way poorly aligned with fundamental values.

The Theoretical Relationship Between FVA, Liquidity Pricing, and Risk Contagion: The Industrial Bonds Example

So how does FVA relate to liquidity pricing and risk contagion in economic models? A simplified explanation goes something like this: Imagine a world with two independent firms, one of which is a bank (Firm A), and the other of which is an agricultural business (Firm B). The two firms have no economic connection to each other and no commonality other than that both happen hold an important financial asset in common (let's call that asset "industrial bonds"). Now imagine that an isolated economic shock occurs that puts Firm B, the agricultural business, at risk of insolvency and compels it to raise cash. Imagine that Firm B needs to sell some of its assets (i.e., the industrial bonds) in the short term, but faces liquidity pricing when it tries to do so. As a result, when Firm B sells its industrial bonds, it realizes a price well below the "fundamental value," i.e., the discounted present value of their future stream of payments associated with those bonds.

Thus, Firm B takes a loss because of an economic shock plus liquidity pricing. But what about Firm A, the bank? Well, in a world in which Firm A faces no economic shock of its own, and where Firm A intends to hold its own industrial bonds for the long term, and where HCA applies to those assets, the fact of transient liquidity pricing in the market for industrial bonds will have no direct impact on Firm A. In this hypothetical example, Firm A will continue to hold its industrial bonds, secure in the knowledge that their long-term value is unimpaired. As a result, the financial statements for Firm A will be unaffected. But a very different result will occur if FVA is the standard for determining the book value of the industrial bonds. In that hypothetical, Firm A will be compelled to adopt the liquidity prices on industrial bonds that were realized by Firm B, and to apply those prices to its own holdings of industrial bonds on its financial statements. The result is a transmission of risk from Firm B to Firm A, with erosion of asset values on Firm A's balance sheet. Particularly where Firm A is a bank, those eroding asset values could in turn trigger solvency problems for Firm A under regulatory capital requirements, which might thereby lead to further sales by Firm A of industrial bonds into an already illiquid market, further deterioration of asset prices, etc.

Economists have developed elaborate liquidity pricing models that seek to specify this kind of scenario in far more precise terms. For example, Allen and Carletti (2008) formulated an influential model to try to clarify the formal theoretical conditions under which FVA would drive exactly this sort of risk contagion effect. Their work (together with similar liquidity pricing models) suggests that FVA can indeed be a unique vector for risk contagion in some cir-

---

[9]   See, e.g., discussion in Adrian and Shin (2008).

cumstances, at least under appropriate model assumptions. Those assumptions notably include the occurrence of liquidity pricing itself and the notion of economically independent firms or sectors that initially have no direct ties or connections with each other, apart from shared exposure to the same category of assets.

More About Risk Contagion Under the Allen and Carletti Model

To elaborate on the foregoing explanation, we describe some additional features of the Allen and Carletti (AC) model, which portrays the contagion of financial risk and distress across two independent economic sectors, labeled "banking" and "insurance." The AC model specifies the behavior of both sectors during three subsequent time periods: A starting period in which all investment decisions are made in both sectors; a second period in which insurance companies discover that they have experienced large (sector-specific) losses, and hence need additional liquidity to pay off insured customers; and finally a third period, in which the banks pay off depositors who have not withdrawn their funds in the second period. The AC model postulates a lengthy set of conditions and assumptions to explain why the banking and insurance sectors choose to hold a long-run asset in common, despite the fact that the fundamental liabilities of the two sectors are different and uncorrelated.

When an economic shock arises in the AC model such that companies in the insurance sector begin to go bankrupt and to sell their long-run assets, the result is to exacerbate an episode of liquidity pricing, such that the market price for the long-run assets falls. Although the bankruptcy and sell-off of assets in the insurance sector has no direct effect on the banking sector, and although the fundamental value of the long-run assets held by the banks is unimpaired (i.e., the eventual return on the banks' assets should be sufficient to fully pay off their liabilities in the final time period of the model), the application of FVA to pricing the assets nevertheless forces the liquidity pricing for the assets onto bank balance sheets. In turn, the reduction in asset values causes a violation of the regulatory capital constraints for the banks. Per Sapra (2008), the result is to compel insolvency in the banking sector and subsequent downstream liquidations of the long-run assets in a way that further amplifies the effect of liquidity pricing. Sapra notes that this outcome not only demonstrates a risk contagion effect associated with FVA, but also a situation where HCA would have produced superior results for all market participants, since the insolvent banks would have been able fully to meet their obligations to depositors if only they had been able to hold on to their long-run assets until maturity (i.e., in the final time period specified by the model).

Put another way, the key result of the AC model framework is a contagion of risk that drives bankruptcy within the banking sector, and which would not have occurred but for the interaction of FVA with liquidity pricing and regulatory capital constraints for banks.

Lessons About Risk Contagion and FVA

The AC model provides a fundamental insight about FVA and contagion. Under some circumstances, two economically unrelated firms or sectors may find themselves holding a financial asset in common. Where there is no short-term liquid market for selling that asset,[10] and an economic shock that is unique to only one of the firms then compels that firm to sell the asset, the value received by that firm may be a "liquidity price" that deviates substantially from the fundamental value of the asset. The second firm, meanwhile, may be entirely unaffected by the shock that hit the first firm, and may have no intention to sell the commonly held asset in the short run. In practice, though, FVA might compel the second firm to remark its books and to incorporate the liquidity price realized by the first firm onto its own balance sheet. Where the second firm is a bank and is subject to a regulatory capital constraint, the loss of value associated with FVA might compel the bank, too, to sell the asset (to try to raise cash) and, in an extreme case, might threaten the solvency of the bank itself.

There are several important implications to consider here. The first is that the AC model offers a rigorous specification of the conditions under which FVA, *but not HCA*, might drive a risk contagion effect across economically unrelated firms or sectors. FVA, when combined with liquidity pricing, has the impact of compelling firms to recognize losses that otherwise would not be captured on their books and that do not reflect the fundamental value of the underlying assets. By contrast, HCA does not, in theory, pose the same risk contagion problem.

In practice, however, the theoretical argument is not a strong criticism against FVA. In particular, the potential for contagion associated with FVA and liquidity pricing depends, in part, on assumptions about how often liquidity pricing actually occurs and on how the accounting standards respond to it when it does occur.[11] To the extent that liquidity pricing doesn't happen very frequently in the real world, then the corresponding potential for contagion may be small.[12] Moreover, in the real world, accounting standards seek to build in an adaptive response to episodes of liquidity pricing. The emergency FASB guidance on fair value, issued at the height of the crisis in 2008, underlined that FVA valuation techniques may shift during a period of acute illiquidity, such that assets that were previously marked to market may instead

---

[10] Again, a question that arises in passing is, Under what circumstances might there be "no short-term liquid market for selling" an asset (or in other words, a lack of market depth, and of ready buyers and sellers for the asset)? Some possible scenarios include an unrelated economic shock that deprives would-be buyers of the cash needed to purchase the asset in an otherwise thinly traded market, loss of confidence among buyers in the quality or nature of the asset being sold, and broader loss of confidence among potential buyers with regard to market conditions and risk more generally. Also, for some types of nonfungible assets, there might also be limited market depth (and therefore limited liquidity) simply because the assets involved are unique, and each asset sale involves a small pool of sophisticated buyers and sellers who need to assess a sui generis set of risks and asset characteristics under conditions of imperfect information.

[11] The potential for contagion also depends on several other major assumptions, such as the scope of application of FVA with regard to particular categories of financial assets, the availability of multiple alternative categories of liquid assets that banks could choose from in deciding how to raise cash in the short term through asset sales, the degree to which FVA methods truly do involve "marking to market" asset prices, the availability of the central bank to step in and provide additional liquidity during a liquidity crisis, the willingness of bank regulators to be flexible in applying capital reserve requirements during a period of acute liquidity, etc. Many of these real-world complexities are beyond the scope of the AC model to try to address, and may represent violations of the assumptions of the AC model to some degree.

[12] In a different vein, consider that one of the potential drivers of liquidity pricing could be loss of market confidence in the meaningfulness of accounting valuation itself—something that likely did happen in the 2008 crisis. This suggests the possibility of another feedback loop, such that lack of *good* FVA information may sometimes itself be an important precondition for liquidity pricing and subsequent risk contagion. At least one of our interviewees commented on the "chicken-and-egg" quality of trying to puzzle out the relationship between valuation and liquidity pricing in episodes of cascading institutional risk.

be priced by model.[13] That accounting policy suggests a relaxation of the theoretical constraints that drive contagion in the AC model. *In the real world, this accounting policy presumably would have the effect of limiting or moderating contagion in some instances.*[14]

The second implication to consider is that that the AC model, and similar economic models of liquidity pricing, represent a strong exercise in logic: An attempt to formulate a set of well-defined conditions under which FVA itself might serve to drive systemically important risk contagion effects. The fact that the AC model succeeds in doing this does not imply that this scenario is actually commonplace in the real world, or that the drawbacks of FVA outweigh its benefits, or that HCA is a superior accounting standard, even from the limited perspective of safeguarding against systemic risk. The AC model does provide a formal basis for understanding the popular anecdotes about the manifestation of contagion and procyclicality during a financial crisis. It also offers support for the *possibility* that FVA might sometimes contribute to downstream risk-contagion problems in the context of liquidity pricing, and particularly so for banks. But even in the model itself, the effects of FVA on banks are mediated by regulatory capital constraints, and by the pressure that those constraints place on banks to respond adaptively to the loss of value in their asset portfolios. We turn to a deeper examination of the relationship between FVA and regulatory capital constraints for banks in Chapter Four.

How Might HCA Contribute to Systemic Risk Among Banking Institutions?

As we have seen, FVA may be associated with risk contagion under some circumstances. It turns out, however, that there is also a very different way in which HCA may be associated with systemic risk as well.

Imagine a scenario very different from the one postulated by the liquidity pricing models for FVA. Imagine that a large bank holds an asset portfolio that includes a pool of hold-to-maturity residential mortgages. Imagine that those mortgages are subject to HCA valuation on the bank's books, and that there is no acute episode of liquidity pricing going in the market for the mortgages that would have any impact on the bank. On its face, this is a hypothetical situation in which FVA-induced risk contagion is unlikely to pose a problem. Nevertheless, it is possible to identify conditions under which HCA standards, as applied to the pool of mortgages, might in some other fashion contribute to risk accumulation within the bank and, ultimately, to broader risk to the financial system.

The concern here is a situation in which HCA, and not FVA, introduces a distorted picture of the value of the mortgages. Because the historical cost of an asset is not directly respon-

---

[13] See SFAS 157-4 (FASB, 2009d). Of course, this FAS update was adopted after the most acute phase of the 2008 financial crisis, in response to pressure and concerns that the existing FVA standard up to that time might indeed have led some institutions to behave in ways contributing to procyclical asset sales and financial contagion. Again, see summary discussion of public comment in FASB (2009c). Note, however, that whether SFAS 157-4 represented a "good" policy response at the height of the crisis is difficult to assess. In principle, more flexible application of FVA standards during a liquidity crunch might help to prevent some asset sales and a procyclicality spiral, but with the potential drawback of undermining confidence in the meaningfulness of asset valuations, possibly thereby contributing to further illiquidity in asset and credit markets.

[14] Consistent with the foregoing, the actual history of the 2008 financial crisis stopped short of the theoretical systemic "death spiral" of contagion, procyclicality, and liquidity pricing.

sive to shifting prices in markets today, HCA can help to protect against the short-term distortions of liquidity pricing. But HCA may also obscure the information contained in the current market price, when that price actually reflects a genuine reduction in the fundamental value of an asset.[15] In principle (and as we discussed in Chapter Two), HCA standards mandate that asset values be marked down to reflect other-than-temporary credit impairments. But what if HCA accounting for other-than-temporary impairment involves the exercise of judgment on the part of the bank? What if there is room for disagreement about whether any observed impairments to asset value are truly "other than temporary"? And what if executives within the bank believe that external market signals about asset values are misinformed or distorted, such that a seeming disparity between market price and historical cost actually suggests a good buying opportunity with regard to the asset, rather than a reason to mark down the bank's balance sheet and to reduce its exposure?

Under circumstances like these, HCA (especially if carried out ineffectively) could operate to conceal risks and asset impairments that FVA would otherwise make transparent. In fact, HCA might also contribute to the further accumulation by the bank of risky assets in these circumstances, either because the bank views the difference between historical value and the external market as a discount buying window, or because the bank wants to gamble on that possibility. Clearly, as with the AC model of liquidity pricing, this too is a scenario that involves a lot of supporting assumptions. In the real world, though, there is at least some evidence to suggest that several of the larger commercial banks that actually collapsed in 2008 (including Washington Mutual and Downey Savings and Loan) may have followed a similar pattern: succumbing in part to spikes in nonperforming loans and associated credit losses that were previously not recognized by the institutions.[16] The potential under HCA for a bank to accumulate risky loan assets, without recognizing and disclosing credit impairments as being other than temporary, has strong implications for risk management and valuation practice within financial institutions. It also has broader implications for *systemic* risk.

HCA does not drive contagion of risk via eroding asset prices, in the same way that FVA does under the AC model. However, when HCA contributes to institutional risk accumulation, it takes only a few additional assumptions for that problem to become systemic in magnitude. If a bank that falls prey to risk accumulation is itself large enough, and sufficiently networked with important contractual counterparties, then HCA-derived distortions in the value of the bank's asset portfolio could pass any related risks of default through to the bank's counterparties. This scenario could plausibly give rise to systemic effects if the bank, and its accumulation of risk, is large enough. More importantly, systemic effects could also occur if more than one bank falls prey to a similar problem of HCA-induced asset accumulation at the same time,[17] or if a corresponding loss of investor confidence in the veracity of one bank's financial statements sparks a contagious loss of confidence in the statements of other banks. HCA could become the driver of a different "flavor" of risk contagion in the latter instance. And even apart from contagion, HCA may nevertheless be a key factor in institutional risk

---

[15]   For example, reduced asset values associated with credit defaults, which degrade the discounted present value of the future stream of payments that those assets will realize.

[16]   See discussion in SEC (2008), pp. 117–136.

[17]   Systemic effects could also be exacerbated if HCA-induced risk accumulation has the effect of distorting market pricing signals for a category of assets, so that financial institutions accumulate more risk over a longer period, prior to a crash or market correction.

accumulation, in a manner that can then become systemic by virtue of other elements of risk correlation or linkage across institutions.[18] As we discuss at length in Chapter Five, there are recent historical episodes that follow this pattern of HCA-induced risk to the financial system as a whole, including the S&L crisis of the 1980s and the LDC crisis of the 1970s.

Concluding Observations

In sum, it's important to recognize that the potential for risk contagion given liquidity pricing is *not* the only criterion for evaluating the relative merits of FVA and HCA. As Sapra (2008) suggests, in the absence of liquidity pricing, FVA may theoretically give a much more accurate picture of the current value of a bank's portfolio of assets than HCA. Moreover, to the extent that HCA may sometimes operate to conceal the accumulation of losses, FVA may provide a much earlier warning signal for loss of value, accumulating risk, and the potential for future insolvency within a bank. Sapra observes that this theoretical case is much in line with what actually happened to many financial institutions during the S&L crisis of the 1980s. By extension, FVA practice may be superior to HCA as a valuation mechanism in some circumstances but not others, or for some purposes but not others.[19] This general observation may also be true in connection with understanding and managing systemic risks to the banking system as a whole.

One question this invites, of course, is whether real-world experience during the financial crisis actually appears to be consistent with these assumptions about the relative merits of the two different approaches. In the next chapter of this report, we turn to that question directly. We also consider more carefully the relationship between bank capital constraints and accounting standards, and the implications of their relationship for systemic risk management and for policy.

---

[18]   We could also hypothesize an event in which a large institution accumulates assets under HCA, fails to account for other-than-temporary impairment of those assets appropriately over a long period of time, and eventually goes insolvent. The insolvency then forces the sale of those assets, which in turn generates a strong market signal about their true value and puts pressure on other institutions and firms to impair their assets accordingly. In principle, we might plausibly observe an FVA-style contagion effect in this kind of situation as well, apart from the transmission of risk by direct counterparty relationships.

[19]   As Sapra (2008) puts it, ". . . mark-to-market accounting would dominate historical cost accounting if, and only if, the welfare losses from contagion are relatively small compared to the welfare losses from inefficient continuation [of potentially insolvent firms] under historical cost accounting" (p. 87).

CHAPTER FOUR

Accounting Standards and Prudential Regulation

The preceding chapter described a set of theoretical conditions under which FVA, but not HCA, can produce contagion of risk across otherwise unrelated firms or industry sectors. An integral part of this liquidity pricing story in the banking sector involves the regulatory capital requirements that determine how much capital a bank needs to hold for a given level of assets. These requirements are also central to many of the anecdotal accounts suggesting that FVA was a primary driver of the financial crisis in 2008.

Any discussion of the relationship between accounting standards and regulatory capital requirements for banks raises basic questions about the nature of the capital requirements, how they work in practice, and how banks might choose to respond adaptively when eroding asset values create a shortfall in capital. The relationship between FVA and regulatory capital requirements also raises the question of whether problems of risk contagion among banks might be best addressed through a modification of accounting standards, a modification of prudential regulatory requirements, or perhaps both.[1] These two structural elements of the financial system are tied together, particularly in giving rise to systemic risk.

We begin this chapter by briefly describing the role of prudential regulators in establishing capital requirements for banks, the nature and scope of those requirements, and the anatomy of how the requirements interact with FVA and HCA standards. We then review some simple examples illustrating how banks might respond when compelled to accommodate FVA-induced write-downs on their assets. We conclude by reviewing recent empirical evidence addressing the extent to which FVA truly did impact bank balance sheets and regulatory capital during the 2008 crisis. Although the available evidence suggests that the direct impact of FVA on bank balance sheets and regulatory capital was actually quite modest, the relationship between accounting standards and prudential regulation may nevertheless be focal for policymakers seeking to address future episodes of systemic risk in the banking sector.

Bank Prudential Regulators and Capital Requirements: The Basics

The prudential regulation of banks in the United States is undertaken collectively by a series of executive branch agencies of the U.S. government, most notably including the Federal

---

[1] In context, it is worth noting that the U.S. prudential regulators enacted a new set of revisions to regulatory capital standards in January of 2010, in response to new FASB standards pertaining to the accounting practice of banking organizations. See U.S. Department of the Treasury, Office of the Comptroller of the Currency (2010).

Reserve and the Federal Deposit Insurance Corporation (FDIC).[2] "Prudential regulation" broadly refers to government oversight of commercial banks and related institutions, intended to protect depositors against the risks of a default that might otherwise threaten their deposits. One of the major regulatory tools deployed to protect against such defaults are formal capital requirements for banks, which operate to establish a minimum mandatory ratio between bank capital and bank assets. At the most basic level, the capital of any institution or corporation can be defined as the difference between its assets and its liabilities:

$$Capital = Assets - Liabilities$$

Thus, by establishing a minimum ratio for bank capital to bank assets, prudential regulators seek to ensure that banks maintain an asset cushion against any potential for insolvency, and an ability to respond effectively in the event that depositors seek to withdraw their money. When combined with supervisory review, capital requirements help regulators to ensure that banks remain well financed to meet their obligations to their creditors.

Two related points deserve mention. First is that the prudential regulation of banks generally applies to depository institutions (i.e., commercial banks) and to bank-holding companies (consolidated financial entities that in 2012 include both commercial and investment banks and their subsidiaries and affiliates), but not to other types of financial services entities that do not serve depositors and are not subject to similar regulation. Although some other types of financial institutions (such as mutual funds and insurance companies) may be subject to analogous forms of oversight and/or capital constraint, the primary focus of prudential regulation in the United States is on banks.[3] A second point to note is that the focus of our Chapter Three discussion of risk contagion is likewise on banks, precisely because they are indeed subject to regulatory capital requirements. As we will explain further below, those capital requirements might compel banks either to sell their devalued assets, or to take other compensatory steps to raise additional capital, in response to falling asset prices. By contrast, other types of nonbank institutions are not subject to capital constraints and, when confronted with a liquidity crunch and a transient loss of asset values, may not face the same regulatory oversight and pressure to raise capital.[4]

Bank Capital Ratios in Theory and Practice

The above summary of prudential capital requirements for banks is greatly simplified, in several important ways. Notably, there are multiple regulatory capital ratios that banks are obli-

---

[2] The Federal Reserve and FDIC share bank supervision and regulatory responsibilities with the Office of the Comptroller of the Currency (OCC) and the Office of Thrift Supervision (OTS) at the federal level. For a description of the collective responsibility and cooperation among these agencies, see generally discussion in U.S. Federal Reserve (2005).

[3] See again Elliott (2010) and Elliott (2009a, 2009b).

[4] There certainly could be other factors, such as counterparty collateral commitments, that might influence nonbanking financial institutions to similarly sell devalued assets during a liquidity crunch. The financial crisis of 2008 certainly offers plenty of examples of the latter phenomenon.

gated to meet, each based on a different formal definition for what constitutes "capital."[5] Also, several of the required capital ratios are specified as a percentage of the *risk-weighted assets* of the bank, such that some categories of assets (e.g., cash) receive far more favorable treatment than do others (e.g., ordinary loans).[6] By implication, this means that regulators have established a considerable preference for favored categories of assets when it comes to reviewing the adequacy of bank capital. Finally, there is also a key link between FVA standards and bank capital requirements to consider, such that only some categories of bank assets (e.g., trading securities) but not others (e.g., loans held to maturity) are typically subject to FVA treatment and related markdowns.[7] In theory, what that means is that (1) liquidity-driven reductions in asset values will only create a regulatory capital constraint to the extent that FVA applies to the assets, and (2) when FVA does apply, there might sometimes be an incentive to convert devalued and risky assets into (more favorably weighted) asset categories such as cash, at least in the context of an acute liquidity crunch.

To elaborate, there are several different required capital ratios that banks must meet under the current prudential regulatory framework. Depending on the specific definition of regulatory capital that applies, the threshold for a robust bank capital ratio ranges between 5 percent and 10 percent of assets for a well-capitalized firm. Table 4.1 lists the three major regulatory capital ratios that apply to banks and shows the threshold values that banks are required to meet in order to be considered "well capitalized," "adequately capitalized," or "under-capitalized," respectively. Failure by banks to meet the required ratios, and particularly to qualify as "adequately capitalized," can trigger various forms of oversight and intervention on the part of prudential regulators.[8]

Table 4.1 spotlights the terms "Tier 1" and "Tier 2" capital in describing the required ratios to bank assets. In a sentence, *Tier 1 capital* refers to equity in the bank (i.e., common stock and some types of preferred stock), which has the lowest priority for repayment in the

Table 4.1
Capital Requirements for Banks Circa 2008

Bank Capital	Ratio of Tier 1 Capital to Risk Weighted Assets (%)	Ratio of Tier 1 and 2 Capital to Risk Weighted Assets (%)	Ratio of Tier 1 Capital to Total Assets (Leverage Ratio) (%)
Well capitalized	6	10	5
Adequately capitalized	4	8	3 or 4
Under-capitalized	< 4	< 8	< 3 or 4
Significantly under-capitalized	< 3	< 6	< 3
Critically under-capitalized	2	2	2

SOURCE: Abstracted from SEC (2008), p. 100.

---

[5]   See Elliott (2009a, 2009b, 2010); SEC (2008); see also regulatory standards defining bank capital requirements codified at 12 CFR Part 208 (Fed) and 12 CFR Part 325 (FDIC) (2012).

[6]   For general background on this point, see *The Economist* (2010).

[7]   See discussion in the appendix to this report. Note also that changes in the fair value of some FVA assets held by banks (e.g., debt securities held "available for sale") do not affect regulatory capital, unless the changes result from an other than temporary impairment.

[8]   See Elliott (2009a, 2009b, 2010).

event of bank insolvency, while *Tier 2 capital* refers to preferred stock and some other types of subordinated debt issued by the bank, which also have a relatively low priority for repayment in insolvency.[9] Taken together, Tier 1 and Tier 2 capital represent the portion of value in a bank's assets that corresponds to the stake of the equity-holders, and which serves to protect the interests of bank depositors and most other creditors in the event of eroding asset values and/or default.[10]

An important point to consider, in reflecting on the thresholds for bank capital requirements as set out in Table 4.1, is that there is a great deal of complexity in detail that is hidden in that table. For example, the application of regulatory risk weightings to assets, for purposes of these sorts of calculations, can involve considerable judgment and subtlety on the part of both institutions and regulators.[11] And in a related vein, the calculation of all of the bank capital ratios depends on accounting information, derived via HCA methods, FVA methods, or a combination of both. To the extent that the underlying accounting of assets is compromised, either by liquidity pricing under FVA, or by failure to account accurately for instances other-than-temporary impairment under HCA, then banks and regulators as a result may face a distorted or deceptive picture with regard to the adequacy of bank capital to protect depositors and creditors.

Interestingly, descriptive data from the Federal Reserve Bank of Chicago (FRBC) Bank Holding Company database[12] suggest that most banks were able to weather the storm of the crisis reasonably well. According to the FRBC data, the average bank in the Federal Reserve System had an average Tier 1 to risk-adjusted total assets ratio of 11.9 percent between 2006 and 2010.[13] This number is noteworthy for being well in excess of the required capital ratio, even during the height of the 2008 financial crisis.

Figure 4.1 provides a more elaborate snapshot of average bank capital levels for a sample of several hundred Federal Reserve System banks during 2005 to 2010. Although the figure does show a general downward blip in capital ratios in 2008, it also shows that the average institution among those sampled was well in excess of required capital thresholds during the period through 2010.[14] In fact, even among the large banks in this sample, the average institution was still well above the regulatory threshold for being "well capitalized," by virtue of its Tier 1 to risk-weighted assets ratio. Only for large banks was there an observed trend, in 2007 and 2008, of eroding capital levels. At least superficially, the trend line in Figure 4.1 does not appear to suggest widespread FVA-contagion-driven insolvency of the sort described by the AC liquidity pricing model.[15]

---

[9]   Such debt is "subordinate" in the sense that other debt-holders have a higher priority claim for repayment if a bankruptcy should occur.

[10]   Elliott (2009a, 2009b, 2010).

[11]   One of our interview respondents told us that the details of this process tend to be far more complicated than is suggested by a simple summary of risk-weights by broad asset categories.

[12]   The FRBC Bank Holding Company database contains quarterly information on capital levels for banks, both during and after the 2008 financial crisis.

[13]   Authors' calculations from FRBC Bank Holding Company data.

[14]   Of course, the trend lines in Figure 4.1 reflected average bank capital ratios across institutions, and there was variation among the institutions observed around those average levels.

[15]   Notably, the trends depicted in Figure 4.1 reflect the fact that most banks held only a small fraction of their balance sheet assets in FVA-denominated categories. See Figure A.1 in the appendix and accompanying discussion. Given that

Figure 4.1
Tier 1 to Risk-Weighted Assets Ratio for Large and Small Banks

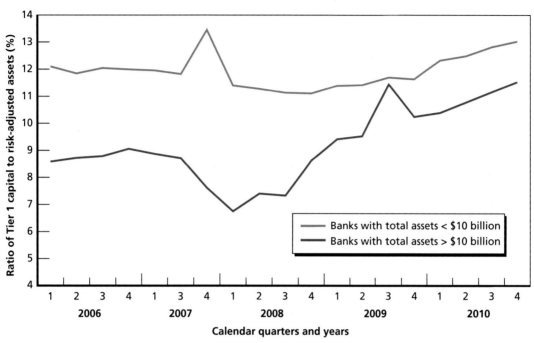

SOURCE: Federal Reserve Bank of Chicago Bank Holding Company Database and authors' calculations.
RAND RR370-4.1

How Can Banks Respond When Facing a Capital Shortfall?

Although banks ordinarily go to great efforts to forecast the value of their assets in order to meet capital requirements, a variety of circumstances might plausibly push a bank into non-compliance, including losses in asset values, errors in risk forecasting, and changes in the regulatory capital requirements themselves. As Admati et al. (2010) point out, there are two basic methods that a bank can then use to return to compliance with its required capital ratios, in any of these circumstances. The first method is that the bank could sell assets. The second is that it could issue new equity.

Consider the simple example of a regulatory increase to bank capital requirements, as illustrated in Table 4.2.[16] Suppose that a bank has a loan portfolio with a value of $100, and deposits and debt used to finance these loans of $90, leaving shareholders with $10 in equity (again, *capital = assets − liabilities*). Suppose further that the regulatory capital requirement (i.e., the ratio of equity to total assets) is 10 percent, so that the bank is exactly in compliance with the regulation. Now suppose that the FDIC increases the capital requirement to 20 percent by regulation. The bank now needs to find a way to boost its ratio of capital to assets. As Admati et al. suggest, the bank has several options available to respond to this contingency. The first

most of the banks (and particularly those with less than $10 billion in assets) did not have substantial exposure to FVA-denominated assets, it follows that eroding prices for such assets would have had relatively modest direct impact on their regulatory capital.

[16] A similar basic spreadsheet example was originally formulated by Admati et al. (2010).

Table 4.2
Different Bank Strategies for Responding to an Increased Capital Requirement

A. Initial Balance Sheet

Assets		Liabilities and Equity	
Loans	$100	Deposits and other liabilities	$90
		Equity	$10
Total	$100	Total	$100
Capital ratio required	0.1		

B. Asset Liquidation (bank sells $50 of its loan assets)

Assets		Liabilities and Equity	
Loans	$50	Deposits and other liabilities	$90
		Equity	$10
Total	$50	Total	$50
New capital ratio required	0.2		

C. Recapitalization (bank issues $10 in new equity, and pays off $10 in other liabilities)

Assets		Liabilities and Equity	
Loans	$100	Deposits and other liabilities	$80
		Equity	$20
Total	$100	Total	$100
New capital ratio required	0.2		

option is shown in panel B ("asset liquidation"), in which the bank liquidates part of its loan portfolio, selling $50 worth of loans and using the proceeds of this sale to pay off $50 worth of debt. This reduces value of the firm overall but leaves the shareholders' equity stake at $10.

By contrast in panel C ("recapitalization"), the bank issues new equity of $10, which is used to pay off $10 worth of liabilities, while the bank's loan portfolio is left unchanged.

Either of these strategies could be adopted by the bank to meet the new capital requirement of 20 percent. In principle, unless the bank has reason to prefer avoiding new equity, there is no intrinsic reason in this example why an increased regulatory capital requirement needs to compel the sale of assets by a bank, or any reduction in its portfolio of loans (Admati et al., 2010).[17] In practice, there are several reasons why banks usually prefer not to issue new equity in these circumstances (including tax disadvantages and the dilution of existing equity holders, among others). Nevertheless, the example shows that even when banks face the need to respond to a binding capital constraint, as in an FVA liquidity pricing scenario, there are multiple strategies that could be pursued to improve bank capital ratios, and that selling assets is not the only possible step.

---

[17] The famous Modigliani Miller theory, outlined by two Nobel Prize–winning economists in the 1970s, asserts that firms will have no intrinsic preference between debt and equity financing, given an idealized set of assumptions. In the real world, those assumptions are almost always violated to some degree, and debt financing is therefore often cheaper than equity. In this vein, economists have postulated a variety of explanations for why banks would typically prefer to obtain additional financing through increasing their debt and leverage, rather than through seeking new equity. See Admati et al. (2010); Elliott (2009a, 2009b); Roberts (2010).

How Can Banks Respond to an FVA-Induced Capital Shortfall?

The situation becomes more complicated when we consider a decline in the value of a bank's assets driven by FVA. The key theoretical question is, How do capital constraints interact with asset write-downs under FVA? The simple answer is that when banks face an FVA-induced shortfall in capital, they may need to sell some assets (say with a low historic cost and an unrealized gain) in order to increase equity. Unlike the case described above, banks will understandably be reluctant to issue new equity when asset values are falling, since equity will likely not raise much money relative to the amount of control existing shareholders must relinquish. This is especially true for highly leveraged banks, in which investors are unlikely to invest in new common stock if they think the firm is going to continue to decline, or perhaps even go bankrupt.

Consider the simple balance sheet in Table 4.3, in which our bank now has two types of assets: loans (traditionally valued under HCA), and a collateralized debt obligation (CDO) that is "held for sale," and hence valued using FVA and mark to market. Suppose as before that the bank has $90 in debt and $10 in equity. At the beginning of the example, the bank successfully meets its 10 percent regulatory capital ratio, and is well capitalized. Then suppose that the CDO asset declines in value by $1, and that the decline is fair valued and deemed "other than temporary" by the regulator. Per panel B of Table 4.3, the value of the CDO now falls to $19, while the value of shareholder equity drops to $9 (thereby absorbing the $1 decline in the value of the bank's assets). But now the bank has a problem: Its ratio of equity capital ($9) to total assets ($99) is now less than 10 percent, below the regulatory capital requirement that the bank must meet.

What options does the bank now have for returning to compliance with the capital requirement? One possibility is to reduce its asset portfolio, as shown below in Table 4.4, either by selling some of its loan assets or some of its (now depressed) CDO assets. In our simple example, the bank has no *a priori* reason to prefer selling one category of assets over the other.

Table 4.3
Impact of an FVA-Induced Capital Shortfall on Bank Balance Sheet

A. Initial Balance Sheet

Assets		Liabilities and Equity	
CDO	$20	Deposits and other liabilities	$90
Loans	$80	Equity	$10
Total	$100	Total	$100
Capital ratio met	0.1		
Capital ratio required	0.1		

B. Balance Sheet Following a $1 Write-Down in CDO Value

Assets		Liabilities and Equity	
CDO	$19	Deposits and other liabilities	$90
Loans	$80	Equity	$9
Total	$99	Total	$99
Capital ratio met	0.091		
Capital ratio required	0.1		

Table 4.4
Bank Responds to Loss of CDO Value by Selling Loans

Bank Responds to Loss of Value by Selling Loans ($9), Reducing Liabilities ($9)			
Assets		Liabilities and Equity	
CDO	$19	Deposits and other liabilities	$81
Loans	$71	Equity	$9
Total	$90	Total	$90
Capital ratio met	0.1		
Capital ratio required	0.1		

Either way, selling $9 worth of assets makes it possible to pay down $9 worth of liabilities, which will return the bank to compliance with the 10 percent capital requirement. But in real-world practice, the bank might have ample reason to prefer the sale of one type of asset over another. In particular, some categories of assets (such as CDOs "available for sale") will be subject to FVA treatment, while other categories of assets (such as cash or traditional bank loans) will not. In this instance, it may be preferable for the bank to sell the CDOs to reduce its short-term liquidity risk associated with further devaluation of those assets. On the other hand, if the bank believes that the CDOs have only been temporarily affected and may eventually return to their fundamental value, then the bank may have the incentive to hold onto the CDOs and sell the loans instead (at historical cost, plus any appreciation).[18]

Table 4.5 shows an example of a different response by the bank to the loss of value in its CDO. In this instance, the bank has chosen to recapitalize itself by issuing another $0.90 of equity stock and using the cash raised thereby to pay off $0.90 in liabilities (i.e., depositor accounts or other creditors). Now the bank balance sheet once again shows that total assets equal $99, total liabilities equal $99, and the ratio of capital to total assets has now been restored to the 10 percent threshold. Again, the example highlights the fact that a bank, when faced with a modest shortfall in capital, doesn't necessarily have to respond by selling its assets.

Table 4.5
Bank Responds to Loss of CDO Value by Recapitalizing

Bank Responds to Loss of Value by Recapitalizing (New Equity = $0.90)			
Assets		Liabilities and Equity	
CDO	$19	Deposits and other liabilities	$89.10
Loans	$80	Equity	$9.90
Total	$99	Total	$99
Capital ratio met	0.1		
Capital ratio required	0.1		

---

[18] In the real world, the incentive for banks to select one or another category of assets to sell might also be influenced (or magnified) by the risk-weighting that is built into some of the capital requirements themselves, such that some categories of assets (e.g., cash) are favored over other others (e.g., loans) in meeting regulatory capital thresholds. In a similar vein, Merrill et al. (2012) notably found that risk-weighted capital requirements among property-and-casualty insurers, when combined with mark-to-market accounting practice, caused insurers with serious operating losses to sell mortgage-backed assets at "fire sale" prices during the 2008 crisis.

But as we mentioned above, there are a host of practical reasons why banks would prefer to avoid recapitalizing, when the opportunity to sell assets is available as an alternative (e.g., shareholder dilution, performance-based executive compensation tied to equity performance).

Finally, note that for banks that are highly leveraged to begin with, there may be no good options for responding to a serious drop in asset values. Consider again Table 4.3 (the base case), and then imagine an example in which the value of CDO assets declines by 50 percent (i.e., losing $10 in value) and in which the equity position of the bank stockholders has consequently been reduced to zero. The bank cannot now sell assets in order to return to compliance with the regulatory capital ratio. The initial decline in asset value is simply too great, and the bank's capital has been entirely wiped out at the starting line. The example showcases that given high initial leverage, proportionately small declines in asset values make it easy to violate regulatory capital requirements, and correspondingly difficult to sell sufficient assets to get back into compliance.

In practice, the high leverage ratios for commercial banks make it important for them to be able to predict their asset values, in order to maintain adequate regulatory capital. In part, the need for stable asset valuation and predictable capital ratios explains some of the traditional antipathy of many bank executives (and of bank regulators) to FVA as applied to bank assets. To the extent that FVA leads to more volatility in asset values than do historic cost methods, this makes it more difficult to predict the adequacy of bank capital and to ensure compliance with capital requirements.

What Are the Implications of Bank Capital Requirements, FVA, and HCA for Systemic Risk?

Based on the foregoing, several points about bank capital requirements deserve emphasis. First, regulatory capital constraints for banks are designed to protect creditors and depositors, in part by ensuring that adequate capital is held to cover unexpected losses in bank asset portfolios. Paradoxically, that means that banks may find themselves pressured to sell assets, or otherwise respond to a capital shortfall, well before reaching the point of actual insolvency. When a bank is confronted with the need to strengthen its capital ratios, there is more than one possible strategy that it could employ—but clearly, sales of assets are an important tactic for shoring up capital. In a situation in which liquidity pricing obtains, regulatory capital requirements could have the effect of nudging banks to sell assets that they otherwise would not sell, because the requirements create immediate pressure to rebalance the books to maintain adequate capital.[19] Furthermore, because some bank capital requirements involve calculations based on risk-weighted assets and favor less risky types of assets in the portfolio (e.g., cash) over more risky ones (e.g., loans), there may be additional pressure on banks to preferentially liquidate some types of assets over others.

---

[19] Note, however, that liquidity pricing may also have an effect on *which* specific assets a bank chooses to sell when placed under pressure to maintain its regulatory capital. To the extent that a bank can choose between selling relatively liquid assets (i.e., those for which current market prices accurately reflect long-run value) as opposed to illiquid assets (i.e., those for which current market prices do not accurately reflect long-run value), then there's an incentive to sell the liquid assets and hold onto the illiquid ones. Assuming this incentive holds true in the real world, then it could tend to act as a brake against spirals of procyclical selling of illiquid assets.

How do FVA standards relate to all of this? The major intersection between FVA and bank capital requirements involves the liquidity pricing models of contagion that we discussed in Chapter Three. When FVA applies to bank assets, and when liquidity pricing also applies, the theoretical result can be to compel banks to reprice their assets in a way not consistent with fundamental value,[20] such that shortfalls in regulatory capital arise.[21] In turn, that creates pressure to sell bank assets to ensure that capital requirements continue to be met, a result that can place further downward pressure on asset prices in an illiquid market. As we discussed earlier, this kind of scenario is theoretically associated with both contagion and procyclicality and, in the extreme case, with potential insolvency on the part of banks. Vulnerability to this cycle, however, depends on the extent to which FVA actually does apply to a large portion of banks' assets.[22] Vulnerability also raises the question of whether shortfalls in bank capital might better be dealt with through relaxed application of FVA standards during a liquidity crisis, or through relaxed application of the regulatory capital requirements themselves. The latter form of relaxation of capital requirements is called "forbearance" in the banking literature, and while it can be explicit, it is more often achieved by allowing distressed assets to remain on banks' books at inflated prices, thereby raising their capital ratios. There is some evidence that both of these types of "relaxation" policies were actually followed during the 2008 crisis.[23]

What about the relationship of HCA to regulatory capital requirements for banks? Here again, HCA is not associated with the same theoretical vector for risk contagion across institutions, under conditions of liquidity pricing. However, HCA does pose the problems of risk accumulation and of concealing unrecognized but other-than-temporary losses in the value of assets that nominally appear unchanged on bank balance sheets. This latter problem occurs when HCA asset values have not been correctly adjusted to reflect other-than-temporary impairment. Where that problem does manifest, it means that superficial compliance by banks with regulatory capital ratios will present a misleading picture of the actual solvency of the banks.[24] As we note in Chapter Five, in several historical instances, this kind of HCA problem has resulted in significant institutional challenges and systemic risk to entire sectors within the financial system. To the extent that policymakers are worried about this sort of risk problem, it might lead to a very different set of policy choices than those involved in trying to deal with FVA-induced procyclicality: e.g., efforts to improve impairment accounting under HCA, to

---

[20]   Again, "fundamental value" conceptually refers to the discounted present value of a future stream of payments associated with an asset.

[21]   In the wake of the 2008 crisis, the GAAP accounting standards codified at ASC 820-10-35-54C et seq. provide guidance for figuring out whether or not episodes of transient liquidity pricing really should figure into the computation of "fair value," in any specific instance.

[22]   As we describe in the appendix to this report, and as the SEC observed in 2008, in fact for many banks in the lead-up to the 2008 crisis, FVA-denominated assets composed only a small fraction of the asset side of their balance sheets. Consequently, direct vulnerability to the cycle would presumably have been low for most of those institutions.

[23]   See, e.g., Diamond and Rajan (2009) and Huizinga and Laeven (2010), who find evidence that the book value of assets claimed by banks exceeded the stock market value of the banks, suggesting that assets were overvalued on banks' balance sheets during the crisis.

[24]   In one of our interviews with a former bank examiner, it was pointed out that misleading bank statements that neglect to adjust appropriately for other-than-temporary impairment, and that conceal accumulated risk in HCA disclosures, are not rare—particularly among institutions that actually go insolvent.

expand the application of FVA principles for bank financial statements, or even to strengthen bank capital requirements themselves.[25]

Perhaps the key insight here is that bank regulatory capital requirements depend on accounting information, and on accounting standards (both FVA and HCA), in order to be effectively applied and enforced. Consequently, any proposed modification to accounting standards, or any change in the fidelity with which those standards are applied by banks in practice, will have ripple effects on the efficacy of prudential regulation for banks. There are some important and subtle implications for risk oversight here. To offer one example, earlier in this chapter we discussed the fact that a bank could respond to a sudden shortfall in its regulatory capital in more than one way, as by selling assets or by recapitalizing. But what about *other* potential responses by banks to a regulatory increase in capital requirements that places them abruptly under pressure? Given the assumption that all else is held equal, then a greater capital requirement would mean that banks somehow have to strengthen their capital ratios. But what if instead some banks were to respond to increased capital requirements with weaker valuation practices, such that non-temporary impairments or losses in the fair value of assets become less likely to be recognized and disclosed? Under this hypothetical, the regulatory intent of stronger bank capital requirements might well be circumvented, if banks chose to substitute less robust valuations in place of actually strengthening their balance sheets. This kind of perversity in accounting practice could plausibly manifest in either an FVA or HCA context—and either way, it would undercut the efforts of prudential regulators to strengthen banks by imposing more stringent requirements for capital.

For purposes of systemic risk oversight, the deep tie between bank regulatory capital requirements and accounting valuation standards (both FVA and HCA) poses a series of important questions for policymakers. What categories of accounting-related risk within the banking system concern us most? How might corresponding changes in accounting standards feed through to the prudential oversight and stability of banks? And how might prudential regulation be improved to address concerns about risk associated with vulnerabilities in accounting information? We touch on the answers to these questions in Chapters Six and Seven. In a nutshell, improving the fidelity of both FVA and HCA information, and fine-tuning prudential oversight of the institutional mechanisms that generate it, offers attractive targets for strengthening the financial system and reducing system-wide risks.

Empirical Evidence on FVA and Risk Contagion

As we suggested in Chapter Three, the central premise of FVA liquidity pricing models is to describe a set of conditions under which FVA can contribute to contagion of risk across independent institutions and sectors. In turn, these models lend some formal credence to the anecdotal accounts that have argued that similar FVA effects, together with liquidity pricing in 2008, drove the same kind of contagion and instability among banks in the real world. As we describe in this chapter, those putative effects are tied into regulatory capital requirements for banks, which purportedly had the effect of driving FVA-induced asset sales and contribut-

[25] In fact, the recent Basel III round of reforms to international bank capital standards did focus specifically on the latter point, and on increasing and strengthening institutional capital reserves. See overview discussion in Basel Committee on Banking Supervision (2010).

ing to procyclical erosion of asset prices and bank balance sheets. One key question that all of this invites, of course, is whether there is any empirical evidence currently available to either support or refute the claims that FVA was a major contributing factor in the dynamics of the 2008 financial collapse.

In fact, in the years since 2008, several empirical studies have sought to examine the impact of FVA in the manifestation of risk to banks during the crisis. These studies fall into a couple of broad categories, based on methodological approach. The first category focuses on the proportion of bank assets that are valued using FVA methods, and/or changes in the value of certain asset classes on bank balance sheets, to assess the probable role of FVA in exacerbating the severity of a crisis. The second category focuses on the proportion of a bank's balance sheet that is accounted for under FVA, or canonical events associated with modifications in FVA practice, as predictors of returns to common equity for financial institutions.

The most well-known empirical investigation of FVA in bank balance sheets is the SEC's 2008 report to Congress on mark-to-market accounting.[26] This report examined in detail the proportion of assets for various banks that were valued using FVA. The SEC report concluded that FVA was not a major contributing factor in bank failures that occurred during the crisis, nor did FVA play a large role in the credit crisis. In complementary series of research studies, Laux and Luez (2010) examined the magnitude of FVA assets included on banks' balance sheets and concluded that it was unlikely that FVA contributed to the financial crisis or resulted in massive fire-sale liquidations. The logic in both the SEC report and the Laux and Luez study is simple. In practice, FVA assets represent only a small fraction of most bank assets, and there are numerous safeguards under GAAP and in prudential oversight that are supposed to protect banks from being forced to use distorted asset prices under FVA in calculating regulatory capital. Consequently, the likelihood that FVA-induced erosion of asset portfolios triggers problems in regulatory capital is low. In sum, Laux and Luez (2010) argued that "for U.S. bank holding companies, the effect of fair value changes on bank income and regulatory capital (in booms or busts) is much more limited that often claimed."

In a somewhat different approach, Shaffer (2010) examined the impact of FVA by looking at changes in regulatory capital levels during the crisis, across a sample of large banking institutions. Importantly, large banking institutions tend to utilize FVA for a larger portion of their asset books and balance sheets, in part because they are more likely to invest in complex or illiquid securities, many of which can only be valued using FVA.[27] In a nutshell, Shaffer argued that those institutions, more so than any others, should have experienced the most pronounced effects of FVA on bank capital. By focusing on the magnitude of changes in asset values (for assets subject to FVA) at these banks, Shaffer sought to determine the direct impact of FVA on the computation of regulatory capital. Shaffer found that most banks in his sample experienced only small reductions in regulatory capital associated with FVA-based changes in assets during 2008. On this basis, Shaffer concluded that "the link between fair value and capital distraction is not evident."[28]

---

[26] The report was undertaken in response to a congressional mandate for an SEC study of the role of mark-to-market accounting during the financial crisis, contained in the Emergency Economic Stabilization Act of 2008 (Pub. L. 110-343).

[27] For example, as Shaffer points out, many derivative products have no initial costs, and hence FVA is the only meaningful way to measure and record their current value.

[28] Shaffer further concluded that most of the reduction in regulatory capital resulted from loan loss provision expenses.

Although these sorts of balance-sheet studies of FVA have generally been skeptical about the empirical link between FVA, regulatory capital, and systemic risk, it is nevertheless important to acknowledge that this kind of research approach has some fundamental limitations. In particular, banks tend to hold very little capital relative to other industries, typically 10–15 percent by definitions used for prudential regulatory purposes, but sometimes as little as 3–5 percent by narrower definitions of capital. Put another way, banks tend to be highly leveraged institutions, with large asset books in proportion to their equity capital. By implication, this means that for banks with even small portions of their balance sheets being marked to market, big changes in asset values could nevertheless still have a destabilizing effect on their capital ratios.

Badertscher, Burks, and Easton (2010) went one step further than the SEC, Laux and Luez, or Shaffer in seeking to estimate the impact on regulatory capital and systemic risk of the percentage of assets on commercial banks' balance sheets that were valued under FVA. They, too, found that FVA-induced losses had a minimal effect on regulatory capital, consistent with Laux and Luez's assertion. Badertscher et al. did find some evidence to suggest that asset sales by banks were associated with higher-magnitude FVA write-downs. However, the observed effects were reportedly quite small, and did not appear to manifest on an industry-wide basis. Put another way, according to Badertscher et al., although a distressed bank may sometimes be forced to sell assets due to FVA losses, there was little evidence to suggest that this then triggers a contagion effect.

Event studies or common equity return studies[29] of FVA take a different approach to investigating systemic risk. There are two widely cited studies that sought to examine the impact of the proportion of FVA assets on the value of bank's common equity. The first, by Kahn (2010), focused on FVA as a predictor that a bank's returns during a particular month are in the bottom 10 percent of the bank's equity returns over the full time period (drawing on data for the period from 1988 through 2007). Kahn (2010) also estimated the impact of the proportion of FVA assets on an index of equity returns on money center banks. Various model coefficients in Kahn's study sought to empirically document increased volatility and contagion effects associated with FVA on bank equity returns. Although Kahn did interpret his results as being consistent with these sorts of effects, methodological limitations in his study make his findings susceptible to alternative interpretations not related to the impact of FVA.[30]

Bowen, Khan, and Rajgopal (2010) conducted a more conventional event study, in which regulatory changes to FVA standards were regressed on stock returns. Broadly speaking, they found that the common equity price of banks reacted positively to regulatory events that relaxed FVA standards, and negatively to those that strengthened it—thereby implying that rigorous FVA practice was associated with diminished value to the banks. Here again, though, the results have to be interpreted in light of the proximity of the firms to bankruptcy (or to

---

[29] A "common equity return study" involves an investigation of the returns on institutional common stock, and how the returns vary over time and in response to external events.

[30] There are some reasons for caution when interpreting Kahn's empirical results. In particular, one reason for the increase in FV assets on bank balance sheets documented by Kahn is that during the time period at issue (particularly following the repeal of Glass-Steagall, the term used for several measures in the Banking Act of 1933 [Pub. L. 73-66] that had imposed a legal barrier separating commercial banking and investment banking activities), many banks acquired new trading desks and assets held-for-sale that were valued at fair value prices. Thus, it is possible that Kahn's findings may have had less to do with contagion and increased risk resulting from FVA, but instead increased risk and common shocks from the entry by commercial banks into new asset-trading businesses during the post-Glass-Steagall era.

their regulatory capital constraints). In short, Bowen et al.'s findings mainly indicate that for banks during the crisis, changes in FVA standards that marginally prolonged the life of imperiled banks were viewed as good for common shareholders. This said, Bowen et al.'s results do not tell us how the value of banks responded overall to changes in FVA regulations, since those changes might have increased the potential cost to taxpayers of bailing out debt holders and depositors of troubled institutions.

Taken collectively, the results of the empirical literature on FVA and systemic risk do not provide compelling support that FVA was a major driver of the collapse, or of associated bank insolvencies, in 2008. In particular, available studies analyzing bank balance sheets provide little support for the proposition that FVA-induced write-downs were strongly associated with shortfalls in regulatory capital, or with instances of bank insolvency, during 2008. And although event and return-to-equity studies have generated somewhat more suggestive findings concerning a possible relationship between FVA and institutional and systemic risk, we think that those studies demand very cautious interpretation, in light of the methods and analytical assumptions built into them. Again, such studies can be vulnerable to confounding historical effects not related to FVA-induced risk, and they may neglect to consider the impact of FVA on institutional risks other than from the perspective of equity shareholders.

Concluding Observations

Prudential regulations mandate that banks maintain a minimum cushion of capital (i.e., equity financing), which operates to protect the interests of bank depositors and other creditors and to limit their risk in the event of a default. When a bank finds itself in violation of capital requirements, as through the devaluation of some of its assets, it can then undertake one of several strategies to try to remedy the situation. In contrast to the assumptions of the AC model, the sale of bank assets is only one pathway to achieving this end. Issuing new equity to bolster bank capital (while either commensurately reducing liabilities or increasing bank assets) is another.

In part, our analysis of prudential capital requirements in this chapter involves further specifying the formal conditions under which FVA-driven risk contagion, as described in the AC model, might actually manifest itself. We conclude that although FVA-driven contagion is a legitimate concern, the theoretical assumptions needed to support it in an extreme form are fairly rigorous and may be difficult to meet in the real world if liquidity pricing is usually rare; large segments of banks' asset portfolios are not subject to fair value treatment; and regulatory capital requirements specifically accommodate concerns about liquidity risk by declining to apply FVA and market pricing for important categories of bank assets. Moreover, recent real-world experience seems to support the same conclusion. Despite the controversy over FVA at the height of the financial crisis, available empirical evidence concerning the crisis does not suggest that FVA was a primary factor in driving a positive feedback loop of asset sales, eroding value in bank balance sheets, and violations of bank regulatory capital requirements culminating in widespread institutional insolvencies.

All of this being said, it is also important to acknowledge that FVA-driven risk contagion, in the laboratory sense described by the AC model, is only one of many factors that might have contributed to systemic risk during the 2008 crisis. Could some element of FVA-driven liquidity effects, as mediated by regulatory capital requirements for banks, have fed into the witches' brew of 2008, which also included risk contagion via counterparty relationships, vulnerable but "systemically important" entities, off-balance sheet investment vehicles, wildly inaccurate valuations of credit risk, and broader loss of investor confidence in the integrity of accounting information? Under extreme circumstances like those, could the procyclical impact of FVA on banks' asset sales, and on banks' efforts to maintain adequate capital ratios, have been magnified? The answer is, perhaps. But even so, the impact was not sufficiently strong to suggest substantial FVA influence in the empirical studies that we reviewed earlier in this chapter. Regardless of the empirical evidence on this point, the argument that FVA devaluation of assets was nevertheless a significant element in the crisis has consistently been made by many FVA critics and bank executives, both in public commentary and in the context of our own interviewing on this topic.

In context, it is important to point out that loss of confidence in the meaningfulness of accounting information itself (FVA and HCA) is another channel by which valuation practice might have contributed to systemic instability, and to asset illiquidity and to the freeze-up in trading and credit markets in 2008.[31] To the extent that market participants believe they can't determine the value of assets or the credit-worthiness of their counterparties given standard accounting disclosures, then broad reluctance to engage in transactions may well be a reasonable response. Under such conditions, market-based asset prices may appear to move toward zero, simply because there are fewer and fewer willing buyers and sellers available to maintain the relevant markets.[32] Although FVA-induced procyclicality did not drive large numbers of bank insolvencies in 2008, broader loss of confidence in the fidelity of accounting information provided by banks, and suspicions about embedded and unacknowledged credit risks associated with their assets, may indeed have contributed to illiquidity and to the freeze-up in markets.[33] In turn, loss of liquidity had very significant impact on the stability of the financial system as a whole. Here again, the strength of accounting valuation practice (both under FVA and HCA) could be important to the genesis of systemic risk, even when the formal conditions for an FVA-induced "death spiral" under the AC model are not met.

What are some other important points to recognize concerning the relationship between prudential regulation, accounting standards, and systemic risk? One basic point to recognize is that bank capital requirements are tied to accounting standards, and vice versa, so that changes in one will necessarily have feedback effects on the operation of the other. Although accounting standards are not primarily designed with the interests of bank regulators or bank solvency in mind, revisions to those standards may nevertheless have substantial impact on the calculation of bank capital and on the prudential oversight of banks. By extension, changes in accounting standards could easily have systemic impact on banks and on the financial system, in ways that might affect the plausibility of risk contagion in the style postulated by the AC model. For policymakers, one key implication is that tweaks to regulatory capital requirements, instead of or in addition to modifications to accounting standards, may be an appropriate way to respond to concerns about systemic risk and contagion in the banking sector.

---

[31] Caballero and Krishnamurthy (2008) made a similar but broader observation in suggesting that "a rise in unknown and immeasurable risk . . . is at the heart of the recent liquidity crisis" and in attributing related valuation risk to complex derivatives whose behavior and characteristics under financial stress were not well understood.

[32] Brunnermeier (2009) notably describes a similar illiquidity scenario using somewhat different terminology, with "asymmetric information frictions" leading to a spiral of loss of confidence, illiquidity, and the superficial appearance of eroding asset values.

[33] Again, see discussion in Caballero and Krishnamurthy (2008).

Ultimately, our review in this chapter underlines the argument made by several commentators,[34] namely that neither HCA nor FVA may be consistently superior as an accounting standard in all possible circumstances, even from the standpoint of prudential regulation and guarding against systemic risk in banks. When an immediate liquidation of institutional assets is either contemplated or necessary, then FVA provides critically useful information to investors and regulators and is an appropriate yardstick for determining asset values. But when immediate liquidation is not contemplated or necessary, and when market illiquidity causes asset prices to deviate from underlying fundamental values, then FVA itself could sometimes have the plausible effect of spreading the distortion of prices, and the liquidation of assets, across institutions and sectors. HCA, by contrast, enjoys the benefits of inertia and can be particularly useful as a valuation method for approximating fundamental values when panic or rampant speculation drives liquidity effects in current market prices for assets. HCA, though, is subject to its own potential for distorting effects and can sometimes operate to conceal risks or losses in asset portfolios in ways that escalate risk and that encourage institutions to "gamble for resurrection." In some instances, HCA has also been associated with eruptions of systemic risk in the financial sector, as we will explore in the following chapter through historical case studies on the S&L crisis of the 1980s and on the LDC crisis of the 1970s. In sum, there is probably no single right answer to which accounting standard is more appropriate or helpful for purposes of prudential regulation and risk oversight in banks.

---

[34] Bob Posen is a notable advocate for this point of view. See discussion in Posen (2010).

CHAPTER FIVE

Lessons from Historical Episodes Involving Accounting Standards, Systemic Risk, and Financial Crisis

In Chapters Three and Four, we explored the conceptual links between FVA and HCA accounting standards, prudential regulation, and systemic risk. We also reviewed the recent empirical literature concerning the financial crisis of 2008 and the extent to which FVA-driven risk contagion actually did play a major role in that crisis. Notably, we touched on the conceptual argument for how HCA may sometimes contribute to episodes of financial crisis, risk contagion, and/or the accumulation of undisclosed losses within institutions. Although the links between HCA and systemic risk have not been focal in the 2008 debate, those links have nevertheless been important in several other recent historical episodes of financial crisis.[1] During our interviews, a few respondents notably suggested that the savings and loan (S&L) crisis of the 1980s reflected an example of this latter kind of episode. Another interview respondent suggested that the S&L crisis and other recent historical cases can provide a useful counterpoint for 2008 in seeking to understand how accounting standards and related financial information have played into events of systemic financial risk during recent decades.

In this chapter, we explore two historical cases, other than 2008, that illustrate the role of valuation accounting in instances of financial crisis: the S&L crisis of the 1980s and the less developed country (LDC) debt crisis of the 1970s. We selected these two cases, in part, because several of our interview respondents specifically pointed them out to us and talked about the similarities and differences between these episodes and the 2008 crisis. We also chose to focus on these cases because (1) they are two of the most recent major episodes of financial crisis and systemic risk prior to 2008 and (2) both episodes involved problems of risk accumulation and contagion in the context of *HCA-related* accounting practice, as a contributing factor in the lead-up to crisis. In the discussion that follows, we have compiled summary accounts of each of these historical cases, drawing primarily on a review of literature and historical documents pertaining to them. Where applicable, we have supplemented the historical review with citation and footnotes to relevant comments offered by our own interview participants regarding the dynamics of these crisis episodes, as well as the role that accounting standards played within them.

Our primary aim in this chapter is to identify and describe what role the accounting standards actually played in each of these previous crisis situations. We will also seek to distill one

---

[1] As we observed in Chapter Three, there is at least some evidence to suggest that some of large commercial banks that became insolvent in 2008 may have been vulnerable, in part, due to losses associated with nonperforming loans and, by implication, to the accumulation of unrecognized credit risk in assets held under an HCA accounting framework. See SEC (2008), pp. 117–135.

or more key lessons about the accounting standards and about their relationship to broad risks to the financial system across these situations.

The Savings and Loan Crisis:[2] Forerunner of 2008?

Introduction

In debates over fair value accounting, the S&L crisis has been portrayed as offering a prequel to the 2008 crisis.[3] According to some proponents of fair value methods, S&L institutions during the 1980s generally used HCA in their bookkeeping, did not recognize losses that should have resulted in other-than-temporary impairment to assets on their financial statements, and were consequently allowed to continue operating long after they should have been shut down by regulators.[4] Because faulty accounting artificially inflated the S&Ls' regulatory capital, it is argued that the S&Ls (also known as "thrifts") were therefore allowed and encouraged to make ever-riskier loans. Depositors, protected by federal deposit insurance, had little incentive to monitor the financial status of the thrifts directly, even if they had had independent means to do so. The accounting argument continues: If the loan assets of the thrifts had been pegged to the market (i.e., dealt with under FVA), then the crisis could have been anticipated[5] and the losses reduced. While some elements of this story are indeed accurate, a careful reading of the history of the S&L crisis does not support the superiority of one accounting approach over the other. Instead, it suggests the limits of accounting standards more generally in the face of lax regulation and political pressure. Much as in the 2008 crisis, the origins of the S&L crisis are deeper and far more complex than a simple recitation of the accounting standards might indicate.

The Origins of the S&L Crisis

Politics played a significant role during the S&L crisis.[6] The very existence of S&L institutions found its origins in a political goal: namely, increasing the percentage of U.S. home ownership during the Great Depression. A series of federal laws passed in the 1930s, designed to encourage home ownership by facilitating the availability of mortgage loans, created both the S&L industry and its regulatory structure. In effect, the industry was created to accept deposits, subject to maximum interest rates determined by law, and then to convert those deposits to 30-year fixed-rate loans for the purchase of homes. From its inception, the S&L industry faced a potential mismatch between its assets (long-term home loans financed at fixed rates) and its liabilities (deposits that could be withdrawn on demand).[7] Despite the mismatch, in the post-

---

[2]   For a more detailed account of the S&L crisis, see FDIC (1997).

[3]   See Nissim and Penman (2010) and Breeden (1991).

[4]   See Enria et al. (2004) and GAO (1991).

[5]   Alternatively, if the loan assets of the S&Ls had been subject to more rigorous impairment accounting under HCA standards, then again, the antecedents to the S&L crisis might have become evident much earlier.

[6]   See White (1991). In fact, a case can be made that the S&L crisis and the current financial crisis are less similar because of issues involving accounting standards than because they are both manifestations of U.S. policy toward housing. See discussion in McLean and Nocera (2010).

[7]   The nature of this mismatch, and the potential for ill effects and institutional insolvency, was captured dramatically in the 1946 Frank Capra film *It's a Wonderful Life*, in the run on the Bailey Building and Loan Association that the film depicted.

war period there were very few runs on S&L institutions, due both to deposit insurance and to the general stability of the U.S. housing market during the period.

The problems for the S&L industry began with the dramatic rise in interest rates during the late 1970 and early 1980s, as then–Federal Reserve chairman Paul Volcker reduced the U.S. money supply in order to combat inflation. Thrifts found themselves holding low interest home mortgages as their primary assets, while facing competition for depositors from other types of institutions (such as banks). Unlike the thrifts, the banks did not face statutory interest rate caps and could offer much higher rates of return to depositors. The effects of competition on the S&L industry, and the subsequent loss of depositors, were dramatic and led to a substantial increase in failures among thrifts during the early years of the 1980s.

As shown in Table 5.1, between 1980 and 1983, 118 thrifts failed. For comparison, during the previous 45 years, only 143 thrifts failed.

Deregulation and Oversight Problems Compounded Risk Accumulation in the S&L Crisis

Several factors at this point exacerbated the crisis, beyond the direct impact of the dramatic rise in interest rates. First, the initial response of Congress to the competitive problems facing the S&L industry was deregulation, via the Institutions Deregulation and Monetary Control Act of 1980 (DIDMCA; Pub L. 96-221) and the Garn–St. Germain Depository Institutions Act of 1982 (Pub. L. 97-320). Both pieces of legislation reduced the capital requirements for thrifts, eased restrictions on their activities, and allowed them to enter new lines of lending, including the provision of business real estate loans (which had previously been the exclusive domain of banks).[8] As it turned out, the latter line of business-oriented loans was outside the traditional core activities of the thrifts and proved to be significantly riskier than other S&L activities. Although the intent of Congress in passing DIDMCA and the Garn–St. Germain Act was presumably to stabilize the S&L industry and its access to depository funds, the argu-

Table 5.1
S&L Failures, 1980–1988

Year	Number of Failures	Total Assets ($ thousands)	Estimated Cost ($ thousands)	Number of Supervisory Mergers	Number of Voluntary Mergers
1980	11	1,348,908	158,193	21	63
1981	34	19,590,802	1,887,709	54	215
1982	73	22,161,187	1,499,584	184	215
1983	51	13,202,823	418,425	34	83
1984	26	5,567,036	886,518	14	31
1985	54	22,573,962	7,420,153	10	47
1986	65	17,566,995	9,130,022	5	45
1987	59	15,045,096	566,729	5	74
1988	190	98,082,879	46,688,466	6	25

SOURCE: FDIC (1997).

---

[8] Deregulation at the federal level prompted a number of states, particularly in the southwestern United States, to enact even more liberal laws governing state chartered S&Ls. The states' concern with losing S&Ls to the federal regulators produced what the FDIC has termed a "competition in laxity."

able effect was to increase institutional leverage, while encouraging the S&Ls to accumulate new asset risks through lines of commercial lending outside their traditional area of expertise.

A second factor contributing to the S&L crisis involved lax supervisory oversight by regulators, arguably associated with simple lack of experience among S&L regulators.[9] Prior to the 1980s, there were relatively few failures among thrifts, and those failures were not particularly costly to resolve. As a result, supervisory oversight of the thrifts was decentralized and generally did not examine the safety and soundness of the institutions. Until the 1980s, this lax oversight made little difference to the stability of S&Ls, which following World War II primarily held high-quality portfolios of mortgages through a decades-long period of appreciation in U.S. housing markets. Losses to individual S&Ls were relatively rare during this period, and concerns about broader systemic risk arising from S&Ls were nonexistent. In consequence, the supervision of S&Ls atrophied to a regulatory backwater,[10] arguably equipped to deal with the simple business of S&L oversight prior to 1980, but not the complex new environment of the 1980s following the deregulation of S&L activities.

Enter HCA and Regulatory Forbearance: When Are Asset Impairments Truly "Permanent"?

As the losses among thrifts mounted during the 1980s, another regulatory problem emerged. Many S&L regulators, either due to the unprecedented nature of the crisis or else to political expediency, argued that S&L insolvencies were really only "losses on paper" stemming from abnormally high interest rates, and that when interest rates fell back to more normal historical levels, the financial health of most S&L institutions would be restored.[11] In effect, institutions and regulators alike argued that S&L losses were only temporary; that forcing write-downs of assets would only create paper insolvencies; that closing institutions for these reasons was unwise; and that the solution was to provide S&Ls with some forbearance on capital requirements until the temporary crisis passed and interest rates returned to their historical (lower) levels. In this spirit, the Federal Home Loan Bank Board (FHLBB) decided to forestall S&L insolvencies by lowering capital requirements from 5 percent of insured accounts to 4 percent (in November 1980) and then to 3 percent (in January 1982).[12]

Several commentators have suggested that the expansion of thrifts into riskier business lending practices, as facilitated by deregulation and motivated by new competitive pressures in lending markets, was really the principal contributing factor in driving the S&L crisis.[13] Subsequent losses experienced by thrifts were then exacerbated by unrealistic HCA treatment of loans (i.e., omitting arguably other-than-temporary impairments), thereby allowing borderline-

---

[9]   See FDIC (1997).

[10]   Among other problems, the generally low levels of risk associated with S&Ls and apparent ease of S&L regulation had by the 1980s led to low levels of compensation and limits on staff at the agencies regulating S&Ls—another factor that contributed to less effective supervisory oversight. See FDIC (1997).

[11]   This was an argument eerily parallel to some of the more recent arguments concerning FVA in the 2008 crisis, in setting out reasons why superficial accounting losses on paper weren't in fact "real." In the S&L context, one of our interview respondents expressed the opposite point of view, suggesting that the "losses on paper" argument represented a basic failure in governance and oversight of the S&Ls, in departing from more rigorous accounting treatment that might have helped to stem losses.

[12]   See FDIC (1997). In 1989, the Financial Institutions Reform, Recovery and Enforcement Act of (FIRREA) abolished the FHLBB and moved regulatory oversight of S&Ls to the Office of Thrift Supervision (OTS) in the Department of the Treasury.

[13]   See discussion in FDIC (1997) and White (1991).

insolvent thrifts to continue to compete for depositors by dramatically raising the interest paid on deposits, while channeling the deposits into ever-riskier loans. White (1991) has described this cycle as a "gambling for resurrection"–type problem, whereby moral hazard kicks into the management of a depository institution in which the depositors are insured and equity and institutional capital are low.[14]

The Resolution of the S&L Crisis

Ex post reviews of the scope of the S&L crisis suggest that the eventual magnitude of the bailout was very large. According to one Congressional Budget Office estimate, the Federal Savings and Loan Insurance Corporation (FSLIC), which regulated S&Ls and handled their resolution, was forced to deal with liquidating 489 thrifts at a cost of $180 billion (1992 dollars) between 1980 and 1988.[15] A subsequent U.S. General Accounting Office (GAO) study in 1996 estimated the final cost for resolving the S&L crisis at about $160.1 billion (in 1996 dollars)—about 0.5 percent of 1996 gross domestic product for the United States—making it the most expensive banking crisis in U.S. history prior to 2008.[16]

In the immediate wake of the S&L crisis, the GAO in 1991 studied the role that accounting standards had played in bank failures occurring during the same period.[17] The GAO found that for the 39 bank failures studied, the cost to taxpayers was approximately $9 billion, including collective losses of more than $7 billion among four institutions with assets over $1 billion each. The GAO observed that:

> As a result of the asset valuations FDIC prepared after these banks failed, loss reserves increased from $2.1 billion to $9.4 billion. A major portion of the $7.3 billion deterioration in asset values was not previously reported, because deficiencies in GAAP allowed bank management to unduly delay the recognition of losses . . . and to mask the need for early regulatory intervention that could have minimized losses to the Bank Insurance Fund. (p. 5)

The GAO concluded that abuses in bank accounting practices, and particularly in the recognition of other-than-temporary impairments to assets, had contributed significantly to the failure of early warning mechanisms among prudential regulators, and ultimately to the insolvency of the banks at issue. Although this finding did not apply directly to thrifts, the GAO nevertheless offered its analysis in contemplation of a potential taxpayer bailout of thrifts totaling hundreds of billions of dollars, and with the observation that "accounting and internal control problems have contributed greatly to bank and thrift failures [during the period]" (p. 4).

---

[14] Per White (1991), S&L shareholders, who are at risk of receiving nothing if the institution does not recover, want a riskier loan posture. Depositors, whose interests are largely covered by federal insurance, are happy to accept a higher interest rate on deposits in return for the potential inconvenience of a default and government resolution, and are unlikely to expend much effort monitoring the S&L themselves. The combination of risk-seeking equity-holders, indifferent depositors, and ineffective regulatory oversight of solvency constitutes a recipe for gambling for resurrection, and for seeking out risky assets in the hope that investment returns will once again return the institution to solvency.

[15] See Congressional Budget Office (1993).

[16] See GAO (1996), placing the direct costs at $160.1 billion.

[17] GAO (1991).

Discussion

Clearly, one important element in the story of the S&L crisis involves problems that arose under an HCA accounting framework, such that instances of other-than-temporary impairment to loan assets arguably went unrecognized and unrecorded on institutional books.[18] Moreover, there were also other factors that contributed to lenient accounting treatment of S&L loan assets, at least with regard to the administration of regulatory capital requirements. In particular, S&L capital prior to the 1980s was reportedly augmented by a set of regulatory accounting principles that required less stringent write-downs of distressed assets relative to GAAP. In fact, in the rare instances in which GAAP treatment was more lenient, then S&Ls could revert to GAAP for their accounting practice.[19]

But could improved accounting practices and recognition of losses under HCA (or under FVA) truly have prevented the S&L crisis? Although better and earlier recognition of accumulating impairments in thrift assets might have reduced the size of the eventual S&L bailout, it is unclear whether it really could have prevented the failures in the first place.[20] The accounting treatment of losses (or lack thereof) did facilitate the industry's ability to fight recapitalization in the political sphere. Isaac (2009a) in particular argues that S&L regulators during the 1980s were far less independent than FDIC or other federal bank regulators. Political appointees in the Reagan administration reportedly pushed for deregulation and forbearance toward S&Ls, while simultaneously arguing against spending taxpayer funds on resolving insolvent thrifts because it would increase the federal deficit and debt. Moreover, in further echoes of the 2008 crisis, Reagan administration officials argued against closing a large number of S&Ls or even recognizing losses, for fear of undermining public confidence. The final resolution of the S&L crisis was deferred until the 1989 passage of FIRREA (Financial Institutions Reform, Recovery and Reinforcement Act) and the creation of the Resolution Trust Company, which had the necessary funding to deal with closing down insolvent S&Ls.[21]

The Less Developed Country Debt Crisis[22]

Introduction

The history of the S&L crisis does suggest the potential problems associated with regulatory forbearance by banking supervisors, even if the lessons regarding the role of accounting standards are somewhat more nuanced. A more successful example of regulatory forbearance can be found in the Latin American or "less developed country" (LDC) debt crisis of the late 1970s

---

[18]   Several of our interview subjects commented on the proliferation of poor HCA practice and deliberately distorted impairment accounting as contributing factors in the lead-up to the S&L crisis. One respondent in particular described the experience of reviewing the books of troubled thrifts as an outside examiner, and being shocked by the extent of shortcomings in impairment accounting among institutions that had actually become insolvent.

[19]   The FDIC's canonical history of banking crises during the 1980s cites two specific examples of the lax accounting treatment that applied to S&Ls during this period. First was the FHLBB decision to allow thrifts to recognize a loss over 10 years and to carry the unamortized portion of the loss on the books as an asset. The second was the liberal accounting treatment for goodwill, which had the effect of creating capital for S&L. See FDIC (1997).

[20]   Of course, other factors being equal, a smaller crisis presumably would have been easier for U.S. regulators to manage and resolve.

[21]   See Isaac (2009a) and FDIC (1997).

[22]   See for general overview FDIC (1997) (particularly at Chapter 5, "The LDC Debt Crisis") and Dooley (1995).

and 1980s. The LDC crisis came to a head in 1982, when Mexico's finance minister notified the managing director of the International Monetary Fund (IMF) and the chairman of the Federal Reserve that Mexico could no longer service its debt. The crisis continued to deepen from there, and by October 1983, 27 countries owing $239 billion were in various degrees of default to lenders. For U.S. banks, the crisis was largest in connection with loans to Latin American and Caribbean countries. Sixteen of those countries (including Mexico, Brazil, Venezuela, and Argentina) owed U.S. banks over $176 billion. Of this amount, $37 billion was owed to the eight largest U.S. banks. According to a subsequent history of the crisis authored by the FDIC, this amounted to 147 percent of those banks' capital.[23] In effect, the Latin American default rendered a large portion of the U.S. banking system insolvent for regulatory purposes, which in principle should have required the FDIC to close the banks.

The Origins of the LDC Crisis

The genesis the LDC debt crisis can be found in the expansion of third-world economies in the 1950s and 1960s, as well as in the economic slowdown in the United States in the 1970s, which led U.S. banks to look for new markets in which to expand. U.S. banks during this period notably faced decreased profitability at home, as commercial lending customers moved to other credit sources, such as commercial paper.[24] At the same time, the rise in oil prices in early 1970s created a glut of petro-dollars that were recycled back to industrialized countries in the Eurodollar market. This market provided new deposit funds to U.S. banks, which the banks then lent to LDCs. Although the LDC loans largely originated from money center banks in the United States, they were then sold off as assets to various regional banks, so that LDC debt was spread through much of the U.S. banking system.[25]

The debt-service problems of the LDCs grew as the price of oil rose during the 1970s and the LDCs found they needed an increasing supply of dollars to pay for imported goods. U.S. banks obliged by providing dollar-based loans to the LDCs, to finance their increasing trade deficits during the period. For example, Latin America experienced dramatic increase in debt from about $30 billion in 1970 to almost $200 billion by the end of the decade.[26] About 80 percent of that debt was sovereign, meaning that it had been loaned directly to governments (Reinhart and Rogoff, 2008). Moreover, the terms of the typical sovereign loan, which involved a medium- to long-term contract with a floating interest rate tied to the London Interbank Offering Rate (LIBOR) and reset semiannually, made the LDC debt very sensitive to interest rate changes and to macroeconomic conditions in the United States.

Regulatory Intervention in the LDC Crisis

In contrast to the S&L crisis, the gradual build-up of LDC debt was noticed fairly early on by U.S. regulators. Arthur Burns, then the chairman of the Federal Reserve, commented on the

---

[23] FDIC (1997).

[24] "Commercial paper" broadly refers to unsecured, short-term debt instruments issued by corporations, with fixed maturity of less than 270 days.

[25] For a discussion of the evolution of this aspect of the LDC crisis, in the context of historical financial and banking crisis episodes more broadly, see Reinhart and Rogoff (2008).

[26] World Bank World Debt Tables.

build-up and systemic risk posed by LDC sovereign debt as early as 1977.[27] By the late 1970s, the ability of Latin American countries to service their debt was obviously deteriorating, and increasing oil prices in 1979 exacerbated the problem. By 1979, most Latin American countries had debt service burdens of 30+ percent of export earnings, and several (such as Brazil) had ratios above 60 percent. Nevertheless, Latin American countries continued to borrow (and U.S. money center banks continued to lend), with total Latin American debt more than doubling between 1979 and 1982 (from $159 billion to $327 billion). Not surprisingly with the advent of the Mexican default, U.S. bank lending to LDCs declined significantly: Between 1983 and 1989, money-center bank loans outstanding to Latin America decreased from $56 billion to $44 billion, according to statistics published by the FDIC.[28]

The Mexican default presented U.S. bank regulators with a difficult choice. Given the size of money center and regional bank loans to LDCs, most U.S. banks were technically below their regulatory capital requirements. If regulators forced the banks to write down their LDC loans even to an optimistically impaired price for the sovereign debt, then the FDIC would be forced to take over many of those banks, and/or bank regulators would be forced to undertake an expensive, taxpayer-financed recapitalization, since it seemed unlikely that the banks could raise the necessary additional capital from private sources. If, however, loans were kept on the books at their unimpaired historical costs, then banks would not be forced to raise additional capital. U.S. banking regulators opted for the latter course and for forbearance, and did not require that large reserves be set aside on the restructured LDC loans or on the succeeding arrearages (i.e., overdue loan payments) by other nations. The argument for this policy was similar to those made by bank regulators during the S&L crisis: to recognize the losses abruptly would have caused a financial panic. In the actual event of the Mexican default there was no panic, although the problems with U.S. banks did not go unnoticed, as long-term debt ratings of U.S. money center banks fell from uniformly AAA to AA1 and as low as BAA3 (in the case of Manufacturers Hanover), with none of those banks retaining their triple-A rating. During this period, no large U.S. banks failed because of their exposure to LDC loans.[29]

Resolution of the LDC Crisis: Why Did Forbearance Succeed?

Why did regulatory forbearance succeed in defusing the LDC crisis, whereas it produced a far less successful outcome in the case of the S&Ls? The answer likely does not lie in the role of the accounting standards. In both cases, evidence accumulated that the fair value of bank loans was actually far lower than that reported to regulators. The primary difference in the LDC crisis was that money center banks were not allowed by regulators to "double down" on their bad bets and to accumulate additional risky loans without adjusting for impairment (thereby gambling for resurrection with insured deposits). Under the 1989 Brady Plan,[30] the U.S. government explicitly recognized that troubled LDC debtors could not fully service their debts and sought permanent reductions in principal and existing debt-servicing obligations. This recognition forced negotiations between U.S. banks and debtor nations and led to a write-

---

[27]   Arthur F. Burns, "The Need for Order in International Finance," address, April 12, 1977, pp. 4, 5, 13.

[28]   See discussion and descriptive statistics on Latin American debt and U.S. money center bank lending trends in FDIC (1997).

[29]   See FDIC (1997).

[30]   So named after then–Secretary of the Treasury Nicholas Brady, who served during the first Bush administration.

down, rather than simply a restructuring, of the debts. Moreover, U.S. banks were partially bailed out, as substantial funds were raised from the IMF and the World Bank to facilitate the debt reduction.[31] In the end, the Brady Plan agreements between 1989 and 1994 forgave approximately 32 percent of the $191 billion in outstanding loans. These losses were borne by bank shareholders. While substantial, the losses were lower than would have been the case if banks had been forced to write down the loans early on in the crisis, before the intervention of the U.S. government, the IMF, and the World Bank.[32]

What Role Did HCA Play in Forbearance?

What was the primary role of accounting standards during the LDC crisis? The answer is complex. In a hypothetical world in which all bank assets had to be marked immediately to market (or otherwise adjusted to reflect other-than-temporary impairments), the path of forbearance followed by U.S. bank regulators would have been much more difficult to pursue. This notwithstanding, it is also true that stronger HCA practices that more accurately and swiftly accounted for impairments to assets, together with less discretion on the part of banks and regulators in the early phases of the LDC cycle, might have helped to reveal the accumulation of bad debt at a much earlier stage of the crisis, and to better limit the ultimate scope of losses at the outset.

Yet the most important role played by the accounting standards during the LDC crisis, according to several of our interviewees, was that the HCA framework allowed regulators the flexibility not to shut down banks that would otherwise have been insolvent if forced immediately to mark their LDC loans to reflect current prices and actual impairment. The argument presented to us on behalf of this regulatory strategy was that the Federal Reserve and Treasury, along with international financial institutions, planned on finding ways to restructure the LDC debt, and knew that this restructuring would result in losses to U.S. banks being smaller than markets were then anticipating. For political reasons largely related to the negotiating position of the U.S. government, such statements could not be made publicly. Had more rigorous HCA or FVA standards been applied to LDC debt, then the FDIC might have been forced to liquidate the U.S. banks at much greater cost than the eventual realized losses to banks, and certainly at greater cost to taxpayers. It is unclear, however, how well the LDC debt crisis generalizes to other crises. While accounting standards in this instance contributed to regulatory flexibility in the application of bank capital requirements, ultimately much depends on how that flexibility is used by regulators in responding to a specific episode.

Point of Contemporary Comparison: Forbearance on Greek Debt in the Eurozone

Consider by comparison the most recent episode of ongoing debt crisis now occurring in the European Union. As of late 2012, multiple efforts had been made to "bail out" Greece and to reassure the markets that the sovereign debt of several other European countries would indeed be repaid. Several of our interviews suggested that large European banks actively reclassified Greek debt out of their assets "held for sale" (valued under mark-to-market standards) to "held to maturity" (valued under historic cost), where it was claimed that write-downs would be easier to avoid. Given the cost of recapitalizing the banks if they were forced to write down

---

[31] The trade-off for debtor nations was that to qualify for an IMF or World Bank loan, the debtor country had to agree to introduce economic reforms designed to improve economic performance and thereby increase ability to service debt.

[32] See FDIC (1997).

the debt, this too is an example that may involve some degree of forbearance, with bank regulators putatively backing off from rigorous application of capital requirements to rigorously generated accounting information (with full adjustment for other-than-temporary credit impairment associated with sovereign Greek debt). In this sense, at least, the recent Eurozone crisis resembles both the LDC debt crisis and the S&L crisis. With regard to the application of accounting standards, two key questions arise. Ex ante, could more rigorous valuation practices (either under HCA or FVA) have detected the accumulation of risk in Greek sovereign debt more quickly, so as to limit the losses ultimately incurred?[33] And ex post, will regulatory forbearance help in developing a viable debt restructuring plan for the Eurozone, or will it instead involve allowing further accumulation of bad loan assets, possibly abetted by the fiction of poorly applied valuation standards?

It is beyond the scope of this report to analyze in detail the ongoing efforts of European authorities to address and resolve the Eurozone debt crisis. Nevertheless, the similarity between some elements of past historical crisis episodes and the current Eurozone crisis minimally deserves some acknowledgment here. It remains to be seen whether the ultimate outcome, in the Eurozone case, will more closely resemble that of the LDC crisis or the S&L crisis.

Concluding Observations

These historical episodes shed some additional light on the basic relationship between accounting methods and systemic risk. The first point to observe is that both the S&L crisis and LDC crisis episodes involved the application of HCA standards and methods; and more specifically, that both entailed problems having to do with accurately accounting for other-than-temporary impairments to assets within an HCA framework. So one simple takeaway is that episodes of systemic financial risk can indeed occur, and historically have occurred, in connection with HCA practices and assets valued under HCA.

A second point to recognize is that both the S&L and LDC crisis events tie back to our discussion in Chapter Two concerning the relevance of investment time frames in determining an appropriate accounting approach. In both crises, the question of whether impairments to financial assets on paper were "real" and other than temporary, or instead illusory and transient, played into the accumulation of financial risk within and across institutions. Judgments about whether to force impairments onto banks' books in these situations partly related back to lack of rigor in the way that HCA standards had been applied, but also to the appropriateness of a short-term liquidation assumption, in deciding what the relevant value of institutional assets really was. In sum, subjectivity in determining other-than-temporary impairment is a core element in the HCA valuation framework, and it sometimes pulls institutions to adopt a longer-term view on the putative transience of losses (and thus to "gamble for resurrection"), when the alternative is to violate regulatory capital constraints in the short run and thereby to risk insolvency.

Finally, it's also important to recognize that accounting standards can influence both the antecedent conditions that give rise to financial crisis, as well as the flexibility and options that

---

[33] Of course, the situation here is complicated by the fact that some of the accounting problems with Greek debt allegedly originated from financial fraud on the part of the Greek government. See, e.g., discussion in Story, Thomas, and Shwartz (2010).

regulators have in responding post-crisis. The LDC episode, in particular, showcases a situation in which the other-than-temporary impairment of bank assets based on liquidation values could easily have been misleading under HCA, given that central bank authorities eventually did intervene to negotiate and reduce the magnitude of other-than-temporary asset value losses experienced by the banks. Put another way, the HCA accounting framework in this instance allowed the authorities greater flexibility to intervene following the crisis, but also likely contributed to the accumulation of risk in the lead-up to the crisis. Whether on balance it's a good idea to preserve greater intervention flexibility on the part of regulators is an open question to consider. The accounting trade-off in both the LDC and S&L episodes was an eventual realization among regulators and other policymakers that substantial unrecognized credit impairments were concealed on the books of many financial institutions—a result that suggests that earlier discovery of those risks via better accounting and valuation practices might have been possible, and helpful, in managing the risks.

CHAPTER SIX

Implementation and Risk: The Challenges to Doing FVA and HCA Well

One of the themes that arose repeatedly in our interviewing about FVA and HCA is the premise that it is possible to apply both methods poorly, in ways that can generate misleading information about asset values. For example, multiple people commented on the difficulties and challenges associated with applying FVA in the middle of a liquidity crisis, particularly in the abrupt absence of a meaningful reference "market price" to mark to. Others spoke about the problems and subjectivity associated with impairment accounting in an HCA framework. In both cases, the underlying implication was that asset valuation processes can sometimes be vulnerable to inaccuracy, error, or even deliberate distortion. A more subtle theme also arose out of the interviews. In the long-running debate over which of FVA or HCA is "better," there is sometimes an implicit assumption that one or the other approach is being applied perfectly, or else in an idealized, simplified way. Disagreements about the comparative merits of FVA and HCA, given the implied assumption of perfect implementation, neglect a more basic problem: Implementation is often less than perfect. Put another way, there are lots of real-world challenges that can detract from the quality of both FVA and HCA information. In turn, poor-quality accounting information has the potential to exacerbate system-wide risks and problems: risk accumulation, gambling for resurrection, loss of confidence in asset valuations, and contagion.

In the course of our interviews, respondents raised a series of concerns connected to the implementation of FVA and HCA and to problems in institutional governance and controls that can limit the fidelity of FVA and HCA information. Some basic assumptions and limits that qualify the meaningfulness of FVA and HCA information were also identified. We briefly outline the most prominent of these issues below, both to spotlight their connection to the broader debate over the accounting standards and to investigate potential leverage points for strengthening the quality of FVA and HCA information as an avenue for helping to protect against systemic risk.

FVA, HCA, and Challenges in Firm-Level Risk Management

A significant theme that arose in several of our interviews with stakeholders in banking institutions was the role that both FVA and HCA sometimes play at the firm level, with respect to institutional risk management and portfolio analysis practices, above and beyond their relevance to the external valuation of firms and assets. One respondent observed that valuation techniques aren't just important in providing a snapshot to outsiders (e.g., investors) about how much a particular asset is worth, but also in providing a snapshot to *insiders* about how much the asset is worth. Another person observed that the valuation of assets by an institution involves accommodating new information about market prices (under FVA) or credit risks (under HCA), in a process of tracking what the investments are worth over time. "Without good valuation procedures, you don't know what your positions and assets are really worth, or what unacknowledged or unrecognized risks might be eroding the value of the assets," observed one person.

> Managing an asset portfolio in a financial firm requires having a reasonably accurate picture of what the assets are worth, regardless of whether FVA or HCA applies. When a firm neglects to carry out effective valuation practices, or violates the assumptions of its own approach to valuation, the result can be to blind the firm to the true value of the assets that it holds, and potentially to accumulate risk in an unintended way.

A related observation was made that when traders have both a direct interest in the value of assets and influence over the valuation process within a firm, the inherent conflict of interest can result in distorted valuations, accumulation of risk, and lack of transparency and effective oversight within the firm.

Interestingly, these sorts of observations about the relationship between valuation and risk management within firms are confirmed by some of the themes raised by international financial regulators, in their postmortem analysis of what went wrong within major financial institutions during and after the 2008 financial crisis (Senior Supervisors Group, 2008, 2009). The Senior Supervisors Group (SSG)[1] published multiple reports summarizing institutional risk management lessons learned from the crisis, based on intensive interviewing and round-table discussions with nearly a dozen global banking firms and securities organizations. One of the key firm-wide risk management practices that was spotlighted by SSG as distinguishing between institutions that were more successful in navigating the crisis, as opposed to less so, was "the consistent application of independent and rigorous valuation practices across the firm." In particular, SSG observed that more successful firms tended to develop the capacity to conduct in-house assessments of "the credit quality of the assets underlying complex securities, to help value their exposures correctly," and that such firms "sought to use those values consistently across the firm" (Senior Supervisors Group, 2008). SSG offered several other risk-management and oversight lessons learned from the experience of the financial crisis, touching on diverse aspects of firm-level risk identification and analysis, risk controls, and liquidity management, as well as firm practices relating to compensation and governance. Notably, several of these SSG observations and targets for improvement tied back to the robustness of asset valuation mechanisms and practices within the firm.

Valuation approaches are thus related to risks and controls at the firm level, as well as at the financial system level. As history shows, poor firm-level management of risk can sometimes set the stage for subsequent systemic crisis, either by virtue of risk contagion, or via direct counterparty exposures or correlated risks across institutions, or both. Moreover, to the extent that many firms within the financial sector suffer from similar institutional risk management prob-

---

[1]   A group comprising the senior government supervisory authorities overseeing major financial services firms in France, Germany, Switzerland, the United Kingdom, and the United States.

lems associated with faulty valuation practices, those deficiencies could certainly have systemic implications.[2]

Perhaps the most striking point about the findings of SSG is that despite its focus on valuation problems, SSG does not single out either FVA or HCA in addressing the factors that contributed to institutional vulnerability in the 2008 crisis. Another of our interview respondents expressed a strong opinion on this point:

> What distinguished financial firms that did poorly in the 2008 crisis was not whether they primarily applied FVA or HCA to the valuation of their asset portfolios, but rather whether they employed either valuation method *well*. Some firms involved in each of FVA and HCA types of businesses actually performed relatively well through the crisis, in part because they carried out their respective valuation approaches effectively and carefully. By contrast, firms that violated the integrity of their own valuation processes, regardless of which approach applied, tended to inflict serious risk-management problems on themselves.

Audit Integrity and Auditability of FVA and HCA Information

Another major observation that was offered to us about both FVA and HCA approaches is that the quality of the financial information they provide is limited by the rigor of outside review through the auditing process. As we discuss in the appendix to this report, the formal accounting standards issued by FASB provide a common language and set of definitions for what kinds of financial information are supposed to be captured, and how these are supposed to be reported. But it is the independent audit process that (in theory) ensures that those standards are actually followed in practice, and that the information that is thereby generated is valid and reliable. To the extent that auditing works well, and that auditors have the resources and knowledge to be able to carry out effective oversight, financial information should be more meaningful and more reliable as a result. To the extent that auditing works poorly, and that baseline assumptions about the rigor and capability of the audit process are violated, then there is a serious risk that the informational quality of financial statements and accounting practices will be degraded as a result.

In several of our interviews, we heard comments suggesting that both FVA and HCA approaches to valuation may pose serious challenges from the standpoint of independent auditors. With regard to FVA, more than one respondent suggested that auditors sometimes face difficult problems in the oversight of valuation, particularly for assets (or liabilities) for which level 3 inputs[3] are employed in a "mark-to-model" approach. In our interviews, multiple respondents emphasized that it is entirely possible for two different institutions that possess the same asset to adopt different FVA models for valuing it, drawing on different assumptions and level 3 inputs and reaching materially different conclusions about what the value of the asset actually is. Moreover, we were also told that an independent audit firm could potentially uphold both conclusions as legitimate under GAAP, despite the superficial contradiction.

---

[2]   The aim of the 2008 and 2009 SSG reports was, in part, to directly address this link between institutional risk and systemic risk.

[3]   "Level 3 inputs" are unobservable inputs that correspond to assumptions made by a reporting institution concerning the assumptions that market participants would use in pricing an asset. See discussion in the appendix on the hierarchy of inputs to fair value measurement, as specified in GAAP per ASC 820.

Another interview respondent told us that oversight for mark-to-model approaches in FVA frequently involves auditors who are substantially less familiar with the models and their underlying assumptions than are the institutions that develop them: a result that implicitly contributes to weaker audit oversight, and (perhaps) to greater pressure on audit firms to approve the values provided by the institutions. Still another interview respondent with a professional background both in accounting and bank supervision told us that, in his opinion, fair value information contained in the footnotes to financial statements[4] often receives less effective oversight and scrutiny through audit than does similar information presented in the financial statements themselves. Although this point was disputed by other accounting professionals we spoke with, if true it would represent another factor that might reduce confidence in model-based valuations embedded in financial disclosures in some instances.

With regard to HCA, we were told about a different set of problems that auditors sometimes face in reviewing valuations, specifically for banks and financial institutions. In particular, it was pointed out that accounting for other-than-temporary impairments under HCA often involves the exercise of considerable subjective judgment on the part of an institution. One interview respondent observed to us that it is not uncommon for banks to underestimate or understate the extent of other-than-temporary impairment of HCA assets on their books, even without any intent to deceive on their part. Another respondent observed that bank examinations that take place after institutions become insolvent almost invariably reveal a substantial understatement of actual other-than-temporary impairments to assets, concealed by the use of unadjusted historical costs on an institution's financial statements. A third person suggested that accounting for other-than-temporary impairments under an HCA framework represents another area that can be challenging for audit oversight, in much the same way as does FVA involving non-market-traded assets, and for the same reason: Both involve reviewing the reasonableness of the valuation methods and judgments of institutions. In the HCA context, such audit oversight can involve second-guessing the assumptions and model inputs used to determine whether, and to what degree, any observed impairment in asset value really is nontemporary.

In sum, the integrity of the audit process is vital to the quality of both FVA and HCA financial information, and both valuation approaches can pose serious challenges on the audit side. For FVA, those problems manifest most strongly in connection with assets valued by model and with level 3 inputs. And although that probably represents only a small fraction of all instances in which FVA is used under ordinary circumstances,[5] in a situation where acute liquidity pricing arguably obtains, the problems potentially become much larger,[6] and the

---

[4] With regard to the use of FVA in footnotes to financial statements, see ASC 825, "Financial Instruments" (FASB, no date-a; formerly codified at SFAS 107, "Disclosures about Fair Value of Financial Instruments"), which requires the disclosure of the fair value of financial instruments for which it is practical to do so, either in the body of financial statements or in the notes. The impact of ASC 825 is to require fair value disclosures in the notes to financial statements for a range of instruments where fair value is not otherwise required in the body of the financial statements.

[5] E.g., the SEC's empirical review of financial statements from 50 major financial services firms suggested that as of the end of the first quarter of 2008, less than 10 percent of the fair-valued assets of large firms, and less than 5 percent of the fair-valued assets of smaller firms, involved the use of level 3 inputs or assumptions to determine value. See SEC (2008), p. 63.

[6] Again, recall the accounting guidance from SFAS 157-4 in 2009, and its ambiguous instructions suggesting that where liquid markets for an asset have dried up, adjustments to market prices or a model-based approach may be necessary in order to figure out what fair value in an orderly transaction would truly be. Note that the current fair value standard is codified

audit challenges may grow at precisely the time when we would most want audit oversight to be robust. For HCA, the problems tend to manifest around accounting for nontemporary impairment and determinations about what truly is "other than temporary" for this purpose. For both FVA and HCA, the limits of audit as a quality-control device suggest corresponding limits in the quality of accounting information, and in the confidence that can be placed in financial statements by outside users and stakeholders.

Valuation Problems Posed by Complex Financial Institutions and Transactions

Another problem noted in connection with FVA and HCA is the potential for the combination of the two approaches to reduce financial transparency or to create new accounting or risk problems, in a way that goes beyond the application of either approach to value taken in isolation. One paradigmatic case involves a complex financial institution that includes multiple business units, some of which engage in asset trading businesses that use FVA to update prices and to appraise risk, and others of which engage in holding assets as long-term investments that are valued at historical cost. For an enterprise that includes both of these sorts of business units, and in which similar assets can be held in both places but subject to different forms of accounting treatment, the results can be both complex and perverse. One of our interview respondents suggested that a financial services firm that mixes its business in this way can sometimes become subject to an exotic, internal asset accumulation problem, such that its fair value business unit may seek to liquidate an asset by moving it within the firm to the historical cost unit, which then disregards the eroding market price as irrelevant to determining the asset's long-term value. In principle, strong internal controls, risk assessment procedures, and consistent valuation practices ought to help protect firms from this problem. But our respondent observed that even within firms, financial risk tends to flow to wherever oversight practices are least rigorous, and therefore that this kind of problem represents a serious concern for large and complicated financial services entities.

Another interview respondent pointed out a second paradigmatic case of mixing FVA and HCA, in which two independent entities engage in a business transaction that simultaneously involves some aspects dealt with under fair value, and others under historic cost: say, an arrangement that includes the purchase of consulting or investment banking services for cash, and a simultaneous secured loan agreement or asset sale that involves a separate contractual exchange between the counterparties. In this vein, our respondent described to us a series of hypothetical transactions by which an institution might manipulate the use of fair value and historical cost in its own financial statements in order to maximize asset values being recorded at historical cost while reducing the footprint of risk that is subject to fair value disclosure (possibly by moving some aspects of the transaction off the balance sheet). More broadly, our respondent suggested that financial services transactions can sometimes be structured in ways to obtain favorable accounting treatment under FVA and HCA, in much the same way that transactions are often structured in order to obtain favorable tax treatment. The concern with mixed FVA and HCA transactions involves the potential for complex dealings that are primar-

---

at ASC 820, "Fair Value Measurements and Disclosures"—but the same basic problem arises here as well, in valuing assets given an episode of acute market illiquidity.

ily designed simply to evade FVA disclosures that would otherwise apply, and to conceal institutional risks that otherwise would be transparent to investors.[7]

Two related points are worth bearing in mind. The first is that combination of FVA and HCA in a mixed-model accounting framework sometimes can create a potential for financial gamesmanship and fraud, going beyond the risks inherent to either of FVA or HCA taken alone. Second, the combination of the two accounting approaches has important institutional risk management and arbitrage implications to it, which again go beyond the risks associated with either valuation approach viewed in isolation.

When Is a Liquidation Event Relevant to Determining Asset Value?

A central concept that runs through much of the debate over FVA and HCA is liquidation. Under the FVA approach, the value for an asset is ideally determined by a liquidation price in the market—i.e., What could the owner of the asset obtain today, if he or she actually sold it? This is simple and intuitive with regard to assets that actually are traded in the ordinary course of business, and to institutions that typically hold them. The concept of liquidation becomes more complicated, though, as applied to assets that aren't typically traded and that are more commonly held as long-term investments. As some commentators have pointed out, the liquidation value of a long-term asset can still be a very relevant consideration in understanding the financial position of a firm, since it tells you what the firm would realize if it suddenly had a liquidity crunch and found that it needed to sell the asset immediately to raise cash.[8] On the other hand, other commentators have been equally assertive in offering the opposite perspective, which is that a going-concern business that holds investments for the long-term ordinarily won't liquidate those investments in the short run, and particularly so if there is any reason to believe that current market prices represent a departure from the fundamental value of the assets. Consequently, it is argued, fair value based on the current price for liquidating assets in the market is misleading with regard to understanding the true value of the firm's assets.

As we discussed in Chapter Two, institutional business models and investment time horizons are often viewed as having some relevance in determining the appropriateness of FVA versus HCA accounting standards. But there is an additional subtlety to the argument that is easily overlooked. The time frame for liquidating an asset is a key criterion in determining what the value of that asset will be when sold. Likewise, the time frame for liquidating a firm is a key criterion in determining what the value of the firm's assets will be when sold. A firm-level liquidation event, by definition, pins down the value of all assets as of a specific date, because liquidation means that the assets need to be sold *then*.[9] Once a liquidation event is triggered, it

---

[7]   In a somewhat related vein, it is also worth noting that the International Accounting Standards Board (IASB) responded to the 2008 financial crisis by amending IFRS fair value standards, to facilitate the reclassification of assets from fair value to hold-to-maturity under specified circumstances. See discussion in Renders (2009). Here again, to the extent that assets can be moved between FVA and HCA treatment based on exigent circumstances and shifting investor intent, then concerns may arise about accounting transparency and the potential for related manipulation and arbitrage problems.

[8]   In this context, by "liquidity crunch" we mean a sudden and unforeseen shortage in cash available on hand within the institution. The potential for an abrupt liquidity crunch is always a concern in depository institutions, such as banks, since depositors are entitled to withdraw their money at any time in the ordinary course of business.

[9]   Of course, the process of actually working through an institutional bankruptcy, and of liquidating related assets, takes significant time to carry out. Consequently, it may be more accurate to think of a firm-level liquidation event as a limited

no longer matters whether liquidity pricing obtains for an asset—the asset has to be sold, and whatever the market price on that date is, that's the value that the asset will have in liquidation.

The strength of HCA as a valuation method for bank assets is that it recognizes the typical going-concern assumption for banks—i.e., that the institution will not go bankrupt in the ordinary course of business, and therefore, day-to-day fluctuations in market prices for assets may not be the best proxy for long-term value. Unfortunately, that is also a major weakness of the HCA approach. From time to time, banks do become insolvent, and then even those assets that they intended to hold as long-term investments have to be liquidated. As soon as that happens (or becomes a significant risk), the liquidation price for assets immediately becomes highly relevant for understanding the true value of a bank in distress. Several respondents in our interviews pointed this discontinuity out, and noted that the HCA valuation approach embodies a going-concern assumption for banks, while ignoring the possibility of insolvency and a forced liquidation event. For that reason, it was suggested, HCA will often systematically overestimate the true value of a bank's assets, even after making appropriate adjustments for other-than-temporary impairment.[10]

The people we spoke to in interviews expressed a range of different opinions about how best to deal with this kind of liquidation problem, for purposes of valuation accounting. Some felt that both historical cost and fair value disclosures should be provided in bank financial statements, so that both types of information are available to investors. Others noted that an independent assessment of institutional solvency (and liquidation risk) partly depends on a range of nonfinancial disclosures made by banks. Still others favored the idea that FVA disclosures offer the best estimate of what assets are worth in liquidation, and therefore provide an appropriately conservative yardstick for gauging firm value. None of these arguments is conclusive, and they focus more directly on institutional risk than on systemic risk. Nevertheless, this issue serves to underline the relevance of liquidation events and of acute episodes of institutional crisis as points of discontinuity in figuring out which accounting standard may be most relevant for valuing assets. When a bank faces the danger of insolvency, the most appropriate method for valuing its assets may sometimes abruptly shift from HCA to FVA. In turn (and as we discussed in Chapter Five), a similar set of concerns about the relevance and appropriateness of liquidation values can also apply when regulators intervene to manage systemic risk across institutions, particularly in the context of an acute financial crisis.

Endogeneity in Asset Valuation as a Reflection of Market Power

Another important assumption relating to the application of FVA is the notion that asset prices observed in the market are, in some basic sense, independent of the behavior of any particular institution (or person) that might make the observation. When an FVA price really is based on a quotation for the same asset in a liquid market, that implies that the observation of the

---

window in time, rather than as single date, during which assets will have to be sold and their values determined by whatever the going price is during that window.

[10] Note that HCA valuation of a bank's assets may either overestimate or underestimate the value of those assets in a forced liquidation. Overestimates are likely to occur whenever appropriate adjustments for nontemporary impairment have not been made to asset values. By contrast, underestimates may sometimes occur as well, particularly when asset values have appreciated in the market in a manner not adjusted for under HCA.

price is objective and that it hasn't been subject to outside influence or manipulation by any individual firm or market participant. In turn, prices generated by liquid markets are typically believed to reflect the fundamental value of assets (more or less), based on the sum of best available information about those assets, at that time, to all market participants. But what happens when those assumptions about market pricing are violated, and when an institution that seeks to determine an asset price, or to buy or sell an asset, also exercises significant influence over the observed price through its own actions in the marketplace?

One of the implications of illiquidity for an asset is that there are not a sufficient number of buyers and sellers to establish a market-clearing price. Often this situation arises when there are only a handful of institutional participants who either own, or have the means and interest to acquire, a particular asset. Whenever ownership of a financial asset is concentrated in the hands of only a few players, those players may have a disproportionate effect on price, through their own activities in buying or selling. In one hypothetical extreme, an institution with highly concentrated ownership may be able deliberately to manipulate observed prices for the asset, through its own choices about whether to sell it and in what quantity. In another extreme case, a player with equally concentrated ownership may find itself unable to sell assets in the quantity that it desires, because to do so would markedly impact the supply of the asset in the market and, consequently, the price at which supply and demand will equilibrate. These situations of concentrated ownership also raise the likelihood that institutional choices about whether or not to sell assets may sometimes be driven more by concerns about managing valuation, and avoiding deleterious markdowns to assets on the balance sheet, than by underlying concerns about the risk and fundamental value of the assets.[11]

More than one of the interview respondents we spoke with mentioned market power and concentrated asset ownership as potential challenges that can sometimes undercut FVA approaches to pricing, particularly for exotic and illiquid assets. Although this is not a general problem for FVA, it can nevertheless be a serious problem for generating objective "market" prices when it does arise. More broadly, this problem serves as a reminder that FVA prices, even when they do derive from orderly transactions in liquid markets, are not independent of the behavior of buyers and sellers. The correspondence of FVA prices to fundamental value for assets[12] depends on a series of assumptions about the efficient operation of markets, the nature of market participants, and the information available to them. Again, one of the important assumptions here is that ownership of an asset is sufficiently dispersed so that no one market participant winds up with the power to establish or move prices through its own behavior in buying and selling.

Concluding Observations

In this chapter, we reviewed a series of major issues pertaining to FVA and HCA implementation that were raised in our interviews and that go to the quality of information that each valu-

---

[11] The hypothetical cases described above are not really that "extreme" in the real world—the situation of concentrated market power and of endogenous asset pricing occurs whenever financial markets are thin and only a handful of institutional owners are involved in buying and selling a particular category of assets.

[12] Again, the "fundamental value" of an asset notionally corresponds to the discounted present value of the future stream of payments associated with that asset, adjusted to reflect any other than temporary impairment.

ation approach generates. These issues illustrate the challenge involved in implementing either of FVA or HCA well, together with some of the limiting assumptions connected with each approach. Neither FVA nor HCA operates in a vacuum; both approaches depend on support from corporate controls and outside factors (such as independent audit and regulatory oversight) in order to generate good financial information; and both may be important to effective institutional risk management, such that stronger valuation practices and controls may help to safeguard institutions against risk. In a different vein, the observation that FVA may sometimes be subject to an endogeneity and market-power problem, while HCA may sometimes be subject to a problem involving the timing of unanticipated liquidation events, once again underlines that both approaches to valuation involve their own weaknesses and assumptions and that neither is likely to be perfect in the financial information that it generates. How do these various issues relate back to the problems of systemic risk, risk accumulation, and risk contagion? First, systemic risk frequently originates from, or is triggered by, institutional risk. Thus, it follows that weaknesses in FVA and HCA that contribute to institutional risk have the potential to contribute to or exacerbate systemic risk as well. Another part of the answer is that the informational quality of FVA and HCA financial statements is potentially of great importance to prudential and systemic risk regulators, just as much as it is to investors. When the quality of information contained in financial statements is poor or distorted, then regulators too may be impaired in assessing risk and responding to it effectively. A third and related point is the basic observation that regardless of which valuation approach applies (FVA or HCA), there may be an important distinction to draw between institutions that pursue that approach well, versus those that do so poorly or ineffectively. These distinctions in the fidelity of valuation, too, could sometimes have systemic implications and impact, as by undercutting market confidence in the meaningfulness of accounting information or by contributing to episodes of liquidity pricing.

Some of these considerations spotlight corresponding leverage points that might be useful for improving the fidelity of the asset valuation process and, consequently, for reducing risk to the financial system. Strengthening institutional management, governance, and risk oversight processes as these pertain to valuation is an obvious place to start. In a similar vein, finding new ways to strengthen and support independent audit could also help to improve the quality of FVA and HCA information, at least in principle. On a somewhat different note, the oversight of prudential regulators in examining FVA and HCA information offers another possible lever for strengthening the valuation process. As one of our interview respondents noted, the prudential regulators are in a unique position to do "horizontal oversight," comparing model assumptions and asset values across institutions while looking for and investigating outliers. It was suggested that the Federal Reserve's Supervisory Capital Assessment Program (SCAP) operated, at least in part, in a similar way, by imposing common assumptions and requirements during a review of asset and portfolio values. The arguable result of SCAP was to help restore market confidence in the solvency and meaningfulness of accounting disclosures of large institutions, and thereby to help thaw some of the 2008 freeze-up in financial market liquidity.

Because the issues we describe in this chapter offer further insights into how FVA and HCA work in practice, those insights may be very relevant for thinking about policy, and for strengthening the accounting standards and supporting regulatory mechanisms, in order to reinforce the quality of financial information and risk oversight. We expand on this point in the final chapter of this report.

CHAPTER SEVEN

Conclusion and Policy Options

FVA and HCA represent two basic accounting approaches to capturing information about the value of assets. In this report, we examined the long-standing debate over the relative merits of these two approaches and their contributions to risk in the financial system. More specifically, we sought to address two questions:

1. What is the relationship between accounting standards (FVA and HCA) and "systemic risk" (i.e., the contagion of financial risk across institutions, with the potential to destabilize the entire financial system)?
2. What kinds of regulatory, governance, and accounting standards options might policymakers consider to respond to concerns about systemic risk?

Key Findings

We conclude that policymakers concerned with systemic risk in the wake of the 2008 crisis have at times been preoccupied with the wrong set of questions about FVA. In our view, whether FVA caused the 2008 crisis and whether FVA or HCA is a "better" accounting approach are not the most useful questions to focus on. Based on our reading of the available empirical evidence, we conclude that FVA was probably not the primary driver of the 2008 crisis, nor does the history of the crisis comport well with the theory of an FVA-induced, procyclicality spiral of asset sales and markdowns, culminating in widespread bank insolvencies. Meanwhile, the long-running debate over whether one of FVA or HCA is objectively "better" is also likely to be a canard for policymakers whose practical concern is strengthening the financial system against systemic risk.

Based on our review, what seems most clear is that both FVA and HCA can produce useful information, that both approaches can be vulnerable to producing misinformation when not applied rigorously, and that both are capable of contributing to systemic risk under some circumstances. In order to generate high-quality financial information, both approaches depend on rigorous implementation, strong support from governance and controls within financial institutions, and on meaningful oversight through independent audit and regulatory processes. When those supports are weak and the quality of accounting information generated is poor, then both of FVA and HCA can contribute to the accumulation of institutional risk and to various channels for contagion and systemic risk across the financial sector.

Given the foregoing, the key question for policymakers to focus on, with regard to accounting standards and systemic risk is as follows: How can FVA and HCA, and the financial information that *both* methods generate, be improved to better protect against systemic risk to the banking sector in the future? Or, to put in another way, what are some policy options for helping to strengthen the quality of FVA and HCA information to improve prudential oversight and to guard against related systemic risks going forward?

Despite Their Differences, FVA and HCA Also Enjoy Some Underlying Similarities

FVA and HCA involve fundamentally different approaches to valuing assets: The former is most often based on the observed clearing price for an asset in an active market, while the latter is based on the original acquisition price for the asset (as adjusted for nontemporary impairment, if applicable). Interestingly, though, FVA and HCA valuations of financial assets in many circumstances should come close to approximating each other. In particular, FVA and HCA generally should produce the same value for an asset on the initial date when it is acquired. Moreover, if we imagine an ideal world in which FVA and HCA methods are perfect (where FVA really does reflect objective prices in orderly markets, there is no liquidity pricing, HCA is flawless in capturing instances of other-than-temporary impairment, etc.), then the asset values produced by the two methods should continue to approximate each other, and both should correspond to the fundamental value of the asset (i.e., discounted present value of future stream of payments). Setting aside the possibility for unanticipated but real appreciation in an asset, the primary difference between idealized FVA and HCA practice involves transient liquidity effects. FVA in principle captures those effects through market prices, while HCA does not. In the real world, however, both approaches struggle in dealing with liquidity effects. FVA struggles (in part) because episodes of acute market illiquidity raise basic questions about how FVA prices are supposed to be calculated, while HCA struggles because accounting for other-than-temporary impairment presumes that there is an objective way to distinguish between (transient) liquidity risks and (permanent) credit risks. Some element of subjectivity and judgment is difficult to avoid under either accounting approach, when operating in the shadow of liquidity pricing.

One obvious question that this invites is, How can either accounting approach be strengthened to minimize the extent to which it departs from its idealized assumptions? Conceptually, the answer lies at least partly in improving the transparency of valuation practices and methods, in strengthening the institutional processes that give rise to asset valuation, and in reinforcing related control mechanisms, regardless of whether FVA or HCA is the applicable accounting approach. Several of our conversations with stakeholders involved suggestions along these lines. Both accounting approaches are capable of contributing to risk accumulation and contagion problems when they are not practiced in a rigorous way, or when they are compromised by internal conflicts of interest within any given institution. Put another way, both FVA and HCA will always struggle in dealing with liquidity problems. But in principle, each approach can be made more transparent and more robust, consistent with its own basic assumptions. Doing so could broadly help to improve the quality of financial disclosures and statements, and to support more effective risk monitoring and risk management within and across financial institutions.

Moving Beyond the FVA-HCA Debate

From the standpoint of defending against systemic risk in the financial sector, one basic insight about FVA and HCA is that the accounting standards have effects on various stakeholder groups that have little or nothing to do with considerations of systemic risk. Many of the long-standing arguments back and forth about the merits of FVA and HCA are driven by other concerns, ranging from the protection of investors, to the supply of useful information to prudential regulators, to the burdensomeness and cost-effectiveness of accounting requirements for financial institutions and the corporate community. Those various other concerns are important in their own right, and relevant context for understanding the accounting standards, but nevertheless peripheral to questions about systemic risk. In a related vein, it is also worth noting that at least some of the historical debates over FVA and HCA have had the quality of people arguing past each other, rather than directly with each other. In our own interviewing, we initially heard advocates on both sides of the ideological spectrum take strongly opposing positions about the merits and drawbacks of FVA. But when we dug deeper, advocates on both sides acknowledged that each of FVA and HCA could be appropriate and useful in some circumstances. It gradually became clear to us that at least some of the debate (on both sides) tends to involve straw man–type arguments. In particular, some of the most polarized arguments against FVA seemed far more directed against expanding the scope of FVA to cover traditional bank loans, rather than against FVA as an idealized accounting concept, or as it might be applied in a range of other circumstances.

A second basic insight concerning both FVA and HCA is that the information generated by each of the approaches is often imperfect. Both approaches have drawbacks and vulnerabilities; in consequence, users of financial statements that depend on FVA and HCA will always need to qualify their interpretation of those statements, based on their level of confidence in underlying valuation practices. There are several important corollaries to this insight. One is that investors (as well as regulators and other users) will sometimes find themselves making decisions based on imperfect information about asset values, regardless of whether FVA or HCA methods are employed. A second corollary is that the behavior of all market participants needs to be understood in light of the reality of imperfect information: In some extreme circumstances, as during the height of the financial crisis, lack of confidence in accounting information can itself become a driver of market behavior (i.e., panic). A third corollary is that revisions to accounting standards and practices that help to boost confidence in asset valuation, as by making it easier for the users of financial statements to assess the strength of underlying valuation methods, can be an important avenue for empowering investors and others, and for protecting broadly against risk. We return to this point in the policy options that we lay out below.

Prudential Regulation Is a Linchpin That Connects Valuation Approaches with Systemic Risk

A key implication for systemic risk in the financial sector is that the combination of asset valuation, taken together with prudential regulation, is likely more important to the genesis of risk than is either of the valuation accounting approaches (FVA or HCA) when considered by itself. The liquidity pricing models for FVA-based risk contagion typically postulate that banks are compelled to sell devalued assets by virtue of regulatory capital requirements, thereby inducing a positive feedback loop of devaluation to destruction. Meanwhile, the story of sectoral risk accumulation under HCA also involves an element of regulatory oversight, both in the failure to detect unreported asset impairments among institutions in the lead-up to crisis, and then in active regulatory intervention afterward to help financial institutions recover and restructure themselves. In both cases, the role of prudential regulators in monitoring accounting information, applying capital requirements, overseeing financial institutions, and (at times) injecting liquidity is crucial to the manifestation of systemic risk in the banking sector. In sum, it's difficult even to talk about the systemic impact of FVA and HCA without simultaneously alluding to the use of related information by regulators in the oversight of banks.

Another key implication involves the fact that prudential and systemic-risk regulators depend on high-quality financial information about institutions, every bit as much as do investors. The limits of transparency in GAAP financial statements, and the vulnerabilities of FVA and HCA to generating misleading information, have the potential to undermine regulators, much as they do the investor community. Here again, the same point applies both to FVA and HCA information contained in bank financial statements. Better recognition of the limits and weaknesses of valuation, and the development of new strategies and techniques to address those weaknesses, follow as logical priorities for regulators in improving their capability to anticipate and respond to systemic risk. Notably, the Supervisory Capital Assessment Program (SCAP) "stress test" of U.S. banking institutions in the wake of the 2008 crisis can arguably be construed in much the same light: namely, as a forward-looking effort to take available information on institutional solvency and the value of assets, and subject it to a rigorous review based on explicitly pessimistic assumptions about the manifestation of future risks and impairments.

Conclusion and Policy Options

In sum, the question of whether FVA was the primary driver of the financial crisis of 2008 is probably not the most important question for policymakers and standard-setters to consider. Instead, the more focal question involves how both approaches to asset valuation (FVA and HCA) can be strengthened, in conjunction with prudential oversight mechanisms, to better protect against eruptions of systemic risk in the banking sector in the future. By implication, policymakers might think about a range of different options for reforms in institutional practice, accounting standards, and prudential oversight that could help to support that end. Based on our findings in this report, we offer here several related options for policymakers to consider, as avenues with the potential to fortify FVA and HCA information and disclosures, and/or the use of that information in prudential regulation and systemic-risk oversight. We offer these options not as a canonical set of recommendations for eliminating systemic risk associated with the accounting standards, but instead as a set of illustrative leverage points that could help in strengthening the system. In the list that follows, we break these options down into the categories of institutional governance, accounting standard setting, and prudential regulation.

Governance

- *Policymakers should consider new steps to strengthen institutional governance and control mechanisms that in turn support higher-quality FVA and HCA practice within financial firms.* Poor-quality valuation processes were associated with poorer institutional outcomes during the crisis and with various antecedent problems in institutional risk management, oversight, and conflict of interest. The fidelity of accounting information is unlikely to exceed the quality of whatever institutional process generates it. Stronger regulatory guidance and oversight protecting the integrity of the valuation process, and of the management and corporate governance framework that supports it, could help to improve the quality of both FVA and HCA information, and thereby safeguard against risk accumulation and contagion among financial firms.

- *Policymakers could strengthen FVA and HCA approaches to valuation by improving audit oversight in connection with both approaches.* To the extent that auditors face significant challenges in providing rigorous oversight for mark-to-model valuations under FVA, and for the evaluation of other-than-temporary impairments under HCA, policymakers ought to consider ways to strengthen and better support auditors in performing that oversight. We were told that auditors sometimes lack the expertise and resources to fully probe the validity of mark-to-model approaches to valuation, and additionally that the relationship between auditors and their institutional clients can sometimes put further strain on this kind of oversight. The independent audit function is a crucial ancillary support element for making GAAP standards work in practice; to the extent that audit oversight falls short, then the adequacy of financial disclosures may likely be compromised as a result.

Standard Setting

- *Policymakers should consider tightening GAAP standards in connection with both FVA and HCA, to improve the quality of information provided about the impact of liquidity pricing on each valuation approach.* Given that problems with the two approaches tend to arise in the context of liquidity pricing and in accounting for other-than-temporary impairment, it follows that more explicit guidelines for dealing with these problems under the standards might be helpful in producing more consistent financial disclosures. In particular, stronger guidance might help to better specify the conditions under which liquidity pricing contingencies should apply; what disclosures and evidence are required to support those contingencies in the financial statements; and once given those contingencies, what level of detail in disclosure is required concerning the mechanics of valuation for either approach in financial statements.

- *Policymakers should clarify whether financial statements really are required to disclose sufficient detail about FVA mechanics to allow users of financial statements to reconstruct and assess the details of valuation models for themselves.* Current GAAP standards under ASC 820 do seem to require this level of disclosure in connection with mark-to-model valuations and level 3 inputs, but a cursory review of actual fair value disclosures in bank financial statements makes it far less clear what's actually required in practice. The underlying question posed here is, what do the readers of financial statements really need to know in order to independently assess the quality of fair value disclosures embedded in the statements? And what is the optimal level of detail to include in such disclosures, sufficient to support readers of financial statements in this way, without overwhelming them in superfluous detail?

- *Policymakers should consider developing or adding metrics of valuation robustness to augment standard financial disclosures under GAAP.* One way to build on existing FVA and HCA disclosures in financial statements would be to develop better metrics to rate the quality of valuation processes and the data that flow from them. Existing value-at-risk (VaR) based calculations offer one avenue for such a robustness metric, by seeking to quantify the magnitude of observable variation around a point estimate of fair value for an asset portfolio. Complementary metrics might be developed to focus on the quality of the institutional controls and governance that support the valuation process; or on the quality and recency of any reference market prices used in FVA; or on the quality of particular modeling approaches to valuation, based on model sensitivity to changes in underlying parameters, together with any anchoring empirical evidence describing observable variation in those parameters in practice. Further research would need to be done both to validate and make transparent any such robustness metrics in the future.

- *Policymakers and standard-setters should consider adding disclosure requirements to address situations in which market power and other forms of price endogeneity are likely to influence FVA observed market values.* In particular, when the holder of an asset has concentrated ownership and faces a thin market for selling it, then the holder's own choices about whether or not to sell may substantially affect both the supply and market price of the asset. Under those conditions, the potential for deliberate manipulation of FVA prices, or for unintended liquidity effects on price associated with the decision to sell assets, is heightened. These kinds of concerns could be made directly transparent to the users of financial statements, given basic disclosures describing the extent to which concentrated ownership of an asset (or of a relevant category of assets) applies on the part of the institutional holder.

Prudential Regulation

- *Regulators should consider, when strengthening regulatory capital requirements, the potential for perverse asset valuation and institutional governance effects.* The aim in strengthening institutional capital requirements (as under Basel III) is typically to help make banks stronger and more resilient to shocks. For that aim to be met, however, banks actually need to fulfill the more rigorous requirements. To the extent that asset valuation practices are unreliable, opaque, and/or subject to distortion, it may be difficult for outsiders to know how well the strengthened requirements are truly being met. Moreover, where stronger capital requirements are difficult for institutions to meet, that could create pressure for distortion or less rigor in valuation accounting as a way to circumvent capital requirements. Consequently, policymakers should recognize the potential for perverse incentives and the importance of ensuring robust valuation and related institutional safeguards, in order for stronger regulatory capital requirements to achieve their desired effect.
- *Regulators should evaluate whether asset risk-weighting in bank capital requirements has the potential to contribute to perverse risk effects and contagion, in connection with FVA.* The calculation of the ratio of Tier 1 capital[1] to risk-weighted assets favors some categories of assets (e.g., cash) over others (e.g., bank loans) in determining whether regulatory capital requirements are met. One area for concern in systemic oversight is the possibility that risk-weighting of assets might sometimes create an incentive for banks to preferentially liquidate an asset valued with FVA over alternative categories of non-FVA assets, at a

---

[1]   By "Tier 1 capital," we refer to the common stock of a bank, plus its retained earnings.

time when doing so magnifies the likelihood of procyclicality, erosion in asset value, and spreading weakness to the regulatory capital of other institutions. By developing new and better ways to quantify any related risks of contagion, regulators might help to strengthen their own oversight and to reduce systemic risk.

- *Prudential regulators should consider playing a more prominent role in vetting asset valuation practice at large institutions.* The prudential regulators are a key stakeholder group in using FVA and HCA information for risk oversight, and they also occupy a unique position in having influence over, and visibility into, multiple financial institutions at the same time. As illustrated by the 2009 Supervisory Capital Assessment Program, regulatory oversight can be used to investigate and help buttress the fidelity of valuation across institutions, while imposing some common baseline assumptions on related practice. Regulators should consider whether and how prudential oversight of institutional valuation practice might be improved in support of better valuation and risk management processes within financial firms.

An Overview of HCA and FVA

To understand the recent policy debates over FVA and HCA and their relationship to systemic risk, it is important to understand the broad landscape of GAAP financial accounting, the authority by which GAAP principles are formulated, and the anatomy of FVA and HCA as outlined under GAAP.

Who Determines GAAP Standards? The Role of FASB

In the United States, the SEC has statutory authority to establish financial accounting and reporting standards for publicly held companies under the Securities Exchange Act of 1934 (Pub. L. 73-291). Since 1973, the SEC has delegated that authority to the Financial Accounting Standards Board (FASB). FASB is an independent, nongovernmental organization that operates to "establish and improve standards of financial accounting and reporting for nongovernmental entities." FASB maintains a formal codification of GAAP, which serves as the authoritative source of information on applicable accounting and reporting standards in the United States. Although FASB is not itself a government agency and does not follow the requirements of the Administrative Procedures Act (Pub L. 79-404) in promulgating new accounting rules, FASB does have its own formal process for setting new standards. That process includes both analysis and research by its own staff of accounting experts, multiple opportunities for public comment and discussion in connection with proposed revisions to GAAP, and formal deliberations by the FASB itself.

FASB functions as the guardian of robust accounting standards and meaningful financial disclosures for business enterprises throughout the United States. Although FASB operates under authority delegated by the federal government, it is nevertheless an independent organization, and one dedicated to "objectively consider[ing] all stakeholder views" in formulating new accounting policies.[1] The independence and nonpartisanship of FASB is one of its core institutional values, much in line with the integrity of the "decision-useful" financial reports and investor information that the organization seeks to promote. Occasionally, the independence of FASB has also been raised as a point of criticism, when FASB has been involved in making controversial decisions about accounting standards.[2]

GAAP standards as codified by FASB notably represent an important element in the framework for securities regulation in the United States. In particular, the SEC requires that

---

[1] See FASB (no date-b).

[2] See, e.g., Isaac (2009).

all companies publicly traded on a U.S. stock exchange must file quarterly financial statements prepared consistent with GAAP standards. Thus, even though GAAP does not have the force of law in itself, it is nevertheless accepted as authority within the accounting profession and imposed on public companies through the requirements of U.S. securities laws.

What Are Fair Value and Historical Cost Accounting, and When Does Each Apply?

In simplest form, FVA involves the periodic practice of valuing an asset at the price for which it could be sold on the open market, regardless of how much it cost when purchased. By contrast, the HCA approach involves valuing an asset based on its purchase price, less subsequent depreciation and/or impairment. Both sets of accounting standards involve considerable subtlety in practice.

GAAP standards lay out the answers to two basic questions about FVA: (1) When do firms need to use FVA in preparing their financial statements? (2) Assuming that FVA applies, how are firms supposed to compute it?

The question of when FVA applies, particularly in the valuation of financial assets, is dealt with through a series of GAAP standards that identify the types of assets to which FVA applies and the conditions under which it does so. Pursuant to GAAP, FVA is applied to equity securities in most circumstances, to debt securities not purchased with the intent to hold to maturity, to derivatives, and to some (but not all) securitized assets.[3] Under GAAP, the authority that specifically determines when FVA applies is spread through scattered provisions of the codified accounting standards. Broadly speaking under GAAP, in most asset valuation situations in which FVA does not apply to valuing assets, some version of HCA does instead.[4]

How Does Fair Value Accounting Work Under GAAP, and What Does It Require?

Under GAAP, the question of how to do FVA computations is dealt with under the authority of ASC 820, "Fair Value Measurements and Disclosures" (formerly codified at SFAS 157). The basic provisions of the standard were initially released in 2006, and they require that fair value measurements in accounting statements conform to a standard definition and methodology. ASC 820 establishes a common framework for developing fair value estimates and requires expanded financial statement disclosures concerning the assumptions that get built into those estimates. According to the terms of ASC 820, fair value is formally defined as "the price that would be received to sell an asset or paid to transfer a liability in an orderly transaction between market participants at the measurement date."

---

[3] See generally ASC 320 ("Investments—Debt and Equity Securities," formerly codified at FAS 115); ASC 815 ("Derivatives and Hedging," formerly codified at SFAS 133); and ASC 825 ("Financial Instruments," formerly codified at SFAS 159).

[4] To clarify, FASB standards defining GAAP do not seek to exhaustively enumerate all the specific situations where HCA applies. Instead, an HCA approach is implicitly built into many parts of GAAP by default, where FVA or some other valuation approach is not specified instead.

Although FVA is fundamentally defined in terms of the exit price for an asset in an orderly market transaction, many assets potentially subject to FVA treatment under GAAP are not, in fact, exchange-traded. In such instances, it may be difficult or impossible to determine valuation by reference to objective price quotes from an exchange. ASC 820 contemplates this problem in detail and establishes a hierarchy of types of fair value measurement, based on the extent to which the inputs to valuation are observable in the market. Thus, ranked in order from the most to the least observable valuation:

- Level 1 inputs to FVA are "quoted prices from transactions or dealers in active markets for identical assets or liabilities." Level 1 inputs are directly observable.
- Level 2 corresponds to inputs that are observable for the asset or liability, either directly or indirectly (other than level 1 quoted prices). Level 2 assets include quoted prices for similar (but not identical) assets or liabilities in active markets; quoted prices for identical assets but in inactive markets; and market-corroborated or observed inputs pertinent to valuation, other than quoted market prices.
- Level 3 inputs are unobservable inputs that "reflect the reporting entity's own assumptions about the assumptions that market participants would use in pricing an asset or liability." Level 3 inputs are not observable.

Per ASC 820, the valuation techniques used in establishing fair value in any given instance are supposed "to maximize the use of observable inputs, and minimize the use of unobservable inputs." Based on the foregoing, FVA-derived valuations can sometimes be based on highly observable and objective inputs ("mark-to-market"), and sometimes on much more subjective assumptions and unobservable inputs (pejoratively referred to as "mark-to-model"), depending on where in the valuation hierarchy the best available inputs come from.

When the 2008 economic crisis hit, constituents asked FASB for immediate guidance in helping them determine whether or not a market is active, and whether or not a transaction is distressed, for purposes of applying FVA techniques. As a result, FASB at the time issued several additional staff position documents to provide further clarification. The first position (FSP 157-4) helped to address the circumstances of an acutely inactive or illiquid market and allowed firms to depart from observable market prices and to make appropriately adjusted fair value estimates given an acute eruption of market illiquidity. Complementary guidance was simultaneously issued by FASB to address ambiguities in impairment accounting given similar illiquidity for securities either held-to-maturity or available for sale.

How Does Historical Cost Accounting, and Impairment, Work Under GAAP?

HCA records items on the balance sheet using the original amount paid for the asset, less subsequent depreciation. HCA asset valuations are adjusted downward for amortization and for observed instances of other-than-temporary impairment (i.e., when nontransient losses are observed in the fair value of an asset). HCA values are not ordinarily adjusted to reflect unrealized appreciation or increases in asset values over time. Note that determining whether impairment of asset values under HCA is truly "other than temporary" frequently involves an exercise of judgment on the part of a reporting firm or entity. Once having determined that an impairment applies, the mechanics of impairment accounting under HCA may also vary by asset category, and in some instances involve marking down to fair value as the new cost basis (e.g., for hold-to-maturity securities), and in others marking down the asset to reflect probable credit losses (e.g., for hold-for-investment loans).

In Practice, Many Institutional Balance Sheets Reflect a Mixture of HCA and FVA Practices and Assets Under GAAP

Consistent with the foregoing and according to current accounting standards, financial instruments on institutional balance sheets today are valued using a mixed attribute model, which means the valuation method that applies differs depending upon the type of asset and its intended use. The carrying amounts of some assets and liabilities are notably listed on the balance sheet at historical cost, while others are listed at fair value.

Which valuation method predominates? The SEC investigated this question in its 2008 report on mark-to-market accounting, focusing on a sample of 50 important public company financial institutions, including 30 of the largest issuers based in the United States (SEC, 2008). The SEC reviewed the financial statements of these firms at the end of the first quarter in 2008 and found at that time that the average bank held 31 percent of its assets subject to FVA treatment; the average broker-dealer, 50 percent of its assets; and the average insurance firm, 71 percent of its assets. Superficially, at least, this finding suggests that banks carried significant FVA exposure in their asset portfolios but that the majority of their assets were valued at historical cost. It also suggests that both sets of accounting standards are important to the financial statements of banks.

Our review of data from the Federal Reserve Bank of Chicago's Bank Holding Company dataset suggests that in 2006, the typical bank held a far smaller percentage of its balance sheet in FVA-denominated assets than did the 50 banks actually examined by the SEC.[5] Figure A.1 shows our "fair value" measure for selected large institutions in 2006, before the impact of the financial crisis. It suggests that the importance of fair value assets to the institutional balance sheet varied greatly across banks, but that few held 30 percent or more of their assets in FVA-denominated categories. Moreover, in comparing the average observed fraction of FVA assets at "large" institutions (those with assets greater than $10 billion) versus at "small" institutions (those with assets less than $10 billion), smaller banks typically have far less exposure to FVA than do larger banks.

International Financial Reporting Standards Convergence

An important but peripheral issue that came up repeatedly in our conversations with stakeholders was the fact that FASB (the U.S. accounting standard-setter responsible for GAAP) and IASB (the standard-setter responsible for the International Financial Reporting Standards, IFRS) have been involved in a long-term effort since 2006 to harmonize U.S. and international

---

[5] The Federal Reserve Bank of Chicago dataset does not directly specify the fraction of assets subject to FVA treatment at any given institution. However, following the methods used by Laux and Leuz (2010), we used as a proxy the total of trading assets and securities sold under agreements to repurchase. Per Laux and Leuz, since these asset categories are held almost exclusively at fair value, and are the primary categories subject to fair value, they represent a good measure a bank's FVA exposure.

Figure A.1
Fraction of 2006 Bank Assets Held Under FVA for Selected Institutions and for the Average "Large" and "Small" Bank

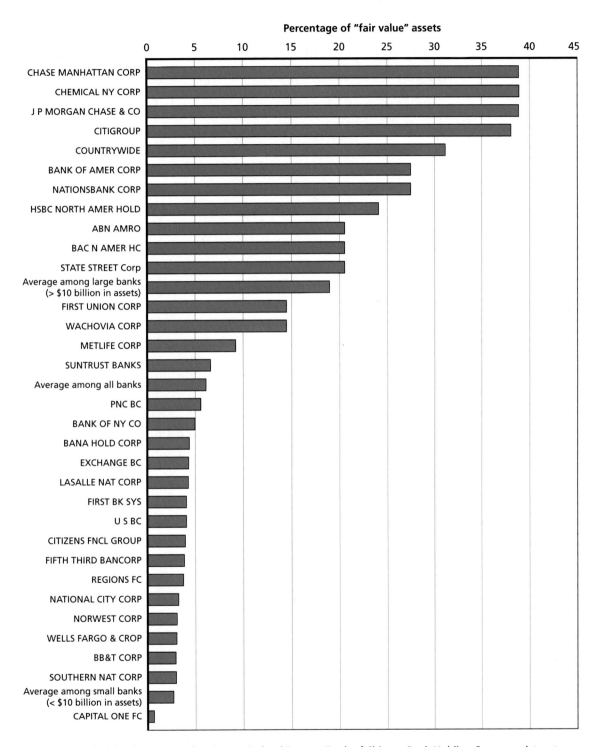

SOURCE: Analysis by the authors drawing on Federal Reserve Bank of Chicago Bank Holding Company dataset.
RAND *RR370-A.1*

accounting standards. Ultimately, the aim is to converge U.S. and international practice under a single set of shared conventions, which (among other things) would eliminate the need for non-U.S. companies registered in the United States to reconcile their IFRS financial statements with GAAP requirements.[6] The IFRS convergence process has now been ongoing for more than five years, and has made substantial progress according to the latest joint report from IASB and FASB.[7] This being said, significant differences in U.S. and international accounting standards remain, and recent comments from IASB and FASB suggest that a new process may be needed to bring the IFRS convergence effort to a conclusion.[8]

According to a recent joint IASB-FASB progress report, fair value measurement and the fair value option are areas where the IFRS convergence effort has now been completed: in particular, through the publication of SFAS 159 (*The Fair Value Option for Financial Assets and Liabilities*) in 2007, and through the publication of IFRS 10 (*Fair Value Measurement*) in 2011. The latter document notably establishes how fair value measurement is supposed to be conducted under IFRS, and substantially converges with the GAAP standard ASC 820 ("Fair Value Measurement and Disclosures"; originally codified in SFAS 157). Despite the foregoing, many important elements of IFRS convergence currently remain in process, including some that potentially relate to when FVA standards apply under IFRS, or else to methods of accounting for other-than-temporary impairment under IFRS. Specific, related ongoing IFRS convergence projects are now focusing on the topics of financial instruments and of impairment accounting.

For current purposes, the details of IFRS convergence, and of relevant international accounting standards, are beyond the scope of the current report to address in detail. Three points are worth keeping in mind, however. First is that concerns about systemic risk and accounting standards implicate both U.S. and non-U.S. banks, financial institutions, and accounting standard-setters. To the extent that GAAP and IFRS diverge from each other, particularly in the way that they deal with FVA and HCA, then that is likely to be an important subtlety in understanding how risk accumulation and contagion might operate across national boundaries. A second point to consider is that financial regulators, both in the United States and elsewhere, share similar responsibilities to monitor financial institutions and to protect the stability of the financial system as a whole. However, their ability to do that, and to intervene in crisis situations, may be significantly influenced by the contours of applicable accounting standards, which at present may differ under U.S. GAAP vs. IFRS. Finally, the ongoing efforts to converge GAAP and IFRS underline the reality that accounting standards are not static, but instead evolve over time. Any future revisions to FVA and HCA designed to address systemic risk issues will need to accommodate IFRS convergence, and the likelihood that the GAAP framework will continue to shift as a result of the IFRS convergence process.

---

[6] See discussion in IASB and FASB (2006).

[7] See discussion in IASB and FASB (2011).

[8] *Journal of Accountancy* (2011).

Discussion

For purposes of exploring the relationship between accounting standards and systemic risk, it is important to keep in mind several basic facts about FVA and HCA. In the United States, both of these accounting approaches are enshrined in a formal set of accounting standards called GAAP. GAAP standards and related FASB guidance documents help to answer two questions in regard to each of FVA and HCA: (1) When does that accounting approach apply? (2) How does it apply? With regard to the question of "how," FVA can involve a broad range of very different valuation techniques, depending on whether a given asset is exchange-traded and liquid (in which case direct market quotes may be available) or not (in which case fair value estimates may instead derive from more or less esoteric financial models). By contrast, the mechanics of HCA valuation are relatively straightforward to understand, with the exception of accounting for nontemporary impairments.

Our review of the basics of accounting standards here deliberately omits much of the complexity that attaches to FVA and HCA standards on paper, much less in practice. So for example, much of the discussion here has implicitly focused on the impact of asset valuation on firm balance sheets, and not on the implications of HCA vs. FVA for other financial statements (and in particular, for the income statement). Those additional accounting complexities can be very important, and particularly so for a sophisticated investor seeking to analyze and understand the details of an institution's financial status over time. But for current purposes, it is sufficient simply to recognize some of the basic mechanics of FVA and HCA, their origins in GAAP standards and FASB authority, and their implications for how the valuation of financial assets in firm balance sheets will be undertaken.

Some of the recent notable policy debates over FVA originated from proposals to expand the application of fair value principles within GAAP, partly in an effort to encompass categories of investment traditionally dealt with under HCA (such as hold-for-investment bank loans).[9] Other debates arose from ambiguity in the application of FVA during an acute liquidity crunch (a scenario that specifically occurred during the 2008 crisis).[10] Both of these elements of recent controversy are worth bearing in mind, when exploring the systemic risk implications of the accounting standards. The scope of application of FVA, and its potential tie to liquidity pricing during a crunch, are both highly relevant to theories and arguments that seek to link FVA to systemic risk and to procyclicality in the banking sector. GAAP standards that define FVA and HCA are also notably tied to a series of deeper disagreements and philosophical arguments about financial information, which in turn have contributed to a long-running dispute about the relative merits of the two accounting approaches. We briefly review these points of deeper disagreement in Chapter Two of this report.

---

[9] See FASB (2010). For a summary of public comments and response to the FASB proposal, see Smith (2010).

[10] In the wake of the 2008 liquidity crunch and calls for an emergency suspension or relaxation of FVA standards, FASB notably issued guidance to clarify when and how FVA applies, in a situation where trading markets evaporate. See particularly FAS 157-4 (FASB, 2009c).

References

Admati, Anat R., Peter M. DeMarzo, Martin F. Hellwig, and Paul Pfleiderer, "Fallacies, Irrelevant Facts, and Myths in the Discussion of Capital Regulation: Why Bank Equity Is Not Expensive," Rock Center for Corporate Governance at Stanford University Working Paper No. 86, Stanford Graduate School of Business Research Paper No. 2065, August 2010. As of August 7, 2013: http://www.gsb.stanford.edu/news/research/admati.etal.html

Adrian, Tobias, and Hung Song Shin, "Liquidity and Financial Contagion," *Financial Stability Review*, Vol. 5, No. 11, 2008, pp. 1–7.

Allen, F., A. Babus, and E. Carletti, "Asset Commonality, Debt Maturity and Systemic Risk," *Journal of Financial Economics*, Vol. 104, No. 3, 2012, pp. 519–534.

Allen, F., and E. Carletti, "Mark-to-Market Accounting and Liquidity Pricing," *Journal of Accounting and Economics*, Vol. 45, Nos. 2–3, 2008, pp. 358–378.

———, "An Overview of the Crisis: Causes, Consequences, and Solutions," *International Review of Finance*, Vol. 10, 2010, pp. 1–26.

Allen, F., and D. Gale, "Financial Contagion," *Journal of Political Economy*, Vol. 108, 2000, pp. 1–34.

ASC 820—*See* Financial Accounting Standards Board, 2011.

Badertscher, Brad A., Jeffrey J. Burks, and Peter D. Easton, "A Convenient Scapegoat: Fair Value Accounting by Commercial Banks During the Financial Crisis," *The Accounting Review*, Vol.8 7, No. 1, 2010, pp. 59–90.

Basel Committee on Banking Supervision, "Group of Governors and Heads of Supervision Announces Higher Global Minimum Capital Standards," Basel, Switzerland, September 12, 2010. As of August 7, 2013: http://www.bis.org/press/p100912.pdf

Board of Governors of the Federal Reserve System, Federal Deposit Insurance Corporation, National Credit Union Administration, Office of the Comptroller of the Currency, and Office of Thrift Supervision, "RE: File Reference No. 1810-100—Accounting Standards Update, Accounting for Financial Instruments and Revisions to the Accounting for Derivative Instruments and Hedging Activities," Comment Letter No. 1402, September 30, 2010.

Bowen, Robert M., Urooj Khan, and Shiva Rajgopal, "The Economic Consequences of Relaxing Fair Value Accounting and Impairment Rules on Banks During the Financial Crisis of 2008–2009," working paper, 2010.

Breeden, Richard C., "Thumbs on the Scale: The Role that Accounting Practices Played in the Savings and Loan Crisis," *Fordham Law Review*, Vol. 59, No. 6, 1991, pp. S71–S91.

Brunnermeier, Markus K., "Deciphering the Liquidity and Credit Crunch: 2007–2008," *Journal of Economic Perspectives*, Vol. 23, No. 1, 2009, pp. 77–100.

Bullard, James, Christopher J. Neely, and David C. Wheelock, "Systemic Risk and the Financial Crisis: A Primer," *Federal Reserve Bank of St. Louis Review*, Vol. 91, 2009, pp. 403–417.

Burns, Arthur F., "The Need for Order in International Finance," address, April 12, 1977.

Caballero, Ricardo J., and A. Krishnamurthy, "Musical Chairs: A Comment on the Credit Crisis," *Financial Stability Review*, Vol. 5, No. 11, 2008, pp. 9–12.

Cascini, Karen T., and Alan DelFavero, "An Evaluation of the Implementation of Fair Value Accounting: Impact on Financial Reporting," *Journal of Business & Economics Research*, Vol. 9, No. 1, 2011, pp. 1–16.

CFA Institute, "Comment Letter to FASB re: Proposed Accounting Standards Update: Fair Value Measurements and Disclosures (Topic 820) Improving Disclosures About Fair Value Measurements," File Reference Number 1810-100, FASB Comment Letter #111, October 28, 2009.

———, *Consideration of the Arguments Against Fair Value as the Measurement Basis for Financial Instruments*, September 2010. As of August 7, 2013:
http://www.cfainstitute.org/ethics/Documents/addressing_arguments_against_fair_value.pdf

Cifuentes, Rodrigo, Gianluigi Ferrucci, and Hyun Song Shin, "Liquidity Risk and Contagion," *Journal of the European Economic Association*, Vol. 3, 2005, pp. 556–566.

CNN, "A Greek Tragedy: How the Debt Crisis Spread Like a Virus in 'Contagion,'" September 19, 2011. As of August 13, 2013:
http://news.blogs.cnn.com/2011/09/19/a-greek-tragedy-how-the-debt-crisis-spread-like-a-virus-in-contagion/

Congressional Budget Office, *The Economic Effects of the Savings and Loan Crisis*, Washington, D.C., 1992. As of August 7, 2013:
http://www.cbo.gov/sites/default/files/cbofiles/ftpdocs/100xx/doc10073/
1992_01_theeconeffectsofthesavings.pdf

———, *Resolving the Thrift Crisis*, Washington, D.C., 1993. As of August 7, 2013:
https://www.cbo.gov/sites/default/files/cbofiles/ftpdocs/103xx/doc10378/1993_04_resolvingthrift.pdf

Curry, Timothy, and Lynn Shibut, "The Cost of the Savings and Loan Crisis: Truth and Consequences," *FDIC Banking Review*, Vol. 13, No. 2, 2000, pp. 26–35.

Diamond, Douglas W., and Raghuram Rajan, "Liquidity Risk, Liquidity Creation and Financial Fragility: A Theory of Banking," *Journal of Political Economy*, Vol. 109, No. 2., 2001, pp. 287–327.

———, "Liquidity Shortages and Banking Crises," *Journal of Finance*, Vol. 60, No. 2, 2005, pp. 615–647.

———, "Fear of Fire Sales and the Credit Squeeze," National Bureau of Economic Research Working Paper 14925, April 2009. As of August 7, 2013:
http://www.nber.org/papers/w14925

Dixon, Lloyd, Noreen Clancy, and Krishnan Kumar, *Hedge Funds and Systemic Risk*, Santa Monica, Calif.: RAND Corporation, MG-1236-CCEG, 2012. As of August 7, 2013:
http://www.rand.org/pubs/monographs/MG1236.html

Dooley, Michael P., "A Retrospective on the Debt Crisis," in Peter Kenan, ed., *Exchange Rate Policy and Interdependence*, Princeton, N.J.: Princeton University Press, 1995.

Dwyer, Gerald P., "What Is Systemic Risk, Anyway?" Federal Reserve Bank of Atlanta Macroblog, November 6, 2009. As of August 7, 2013:
http://macroblog.typepad.com/macroblog/2009/11/what-is-systemic-risk-anyway.html

The Economist, "Basil III: Third Time's the Charm?" September 13, 2010. As of August 13, 2013:
http://www.economist.com/blogs/freeexchange/2010/09/basel_iii

Elliot, Douglas J., *Bank Capital and the Stress Tests*, Washington, D.C.: The Initiative on Business and Public Policy, The Brookings Institution, 2009a.

———, *Quantifying the Effects on Lending of Increased Capital Requirements*, Washington, D.C.: The Pew Financial Reform Project, Briefing Paper #7, 2009b. As of August 7, 2013:
http://www.brookings.edu/~/media/Files/rc/papers/2009/0924_capital_elliott/0924_capital_elliott.pdf

———, *A Primer on Bank Capital*, Washington, D.C.: The Brookings Institution, January 28, 2010. As of August 7, 2013:
http://www.brookings.edu/~/media/research/files/papers/2010/1/
29%20capital%20elliott/0129_capital_primer_elliott

Enria, Andrea, Lorenzo Cappiello, Frank Dierick, Sergio Grittini, Andrew Haralambous, Angela Maddaloni, Philippe Molitor, Fatima Pires, and Paolo Poloni, *Fair Value Accounting and Financial Stability*, Frankfurt am Main, Germany: European Central Bank, Occasional Paper No. 13, April 2004. As of August 7, 2013:
http://www.ecb.de/pub/pdf/scpops/ecbocp13.pdf

FASB—*See* Financial Accounting Services Board.

Federal Deposit Insurance Corporation, *History of the Sii Volume I: An Examination of the Banking Crises of the 1980s and Early 1990s*, Washington, D.C., 1997.

Federal Reserve et al.—*See* Board of Governors of the Federal Reserve System, Federal Deposit Insurance Corporation, National Credit Union Administration, Office of the Comptroller of the Currency, and Office of Thrift Supervision.

Financial Accounting Services Board, Accounting Standards Codification, website, no date-a. As of August 13, 2013:
https://asc.fasb.org/

———, "Facts About FASB," web page, no date-b. As of August 13, 2013:
http://www.fasb.org/jsp/FASB/Page/SectionPage&cid=1176154526495

———, *Accounting by Creditors for Impairment of a Loan: An Amendment of FASB Statements No. 5 and 15*, SFAS No. 114, 2008. As of August 13, 2013:
http://www.fasb.org/cs/BlobServer?blobcol=urldata&blobtable=MungoBlobs&blobkey=id&blobwhere=1175820918856&blobheader=application%2Fpdf

———, *Recognition and Presentation of Other-Than-Temporary Impairments*, FSB No. FAS 115-a, FAS 124-a, and EITF 99-20-b, March 17, 2009a. As of August 13, 2013:
http://www.fasb.org/cs/ContentServer?site=FASB&c=Document_C&pagename=FASB%2FDocument_C%2FDocumentPage&cid=1176157362882

———, *Determining Whether a Market Is Not Active and a Transaction Is Not Distressed*, proposed FAS 157-e, April 1, 2009b. As of August 13, 2013:
http://www.fasb.org/cs/ContentServer?site=FASB&c=Document_C&pagename=FASB%2FDocument_C%2FDocumentPage&cid=1176157362858

———, "Proposed FSP FAS 157-e, *Determining Whether a Market Is Not Active and a Transaction Is Not Distressed*—Comment Letter Summary," April 1, 2009c.

———, *Determining Fair Value When the Volume and Level of Activity for the Asset or Liability Have Significantly Decreased and Identifying Transactions That Are Not Orderly*, FAS 157-4, April 9, 2009d. As of August 13, 2013:
http://www.fasb.org/cs/ContentServer?pagename=FASB%2FDocument_C%2FDocumentPage&cid=1176154545450

———, *Proposed Accounting Standards Update: Accounting for Financial Instruments and Revisions to the Accounting for Derivative Instruments and Hedging Activities*, May 26, 2010. As of August 13, 2013:
http://www.fasb.org/cs/ContentServer?pagename=FASB%2FDocument_C%2FDocumentPage&cid=1176156904144

———, *Accounting Standards Update: Fair Value Measurement (Topic 820)— Amendments to Achieve Common Fair Value Measurement and Disclosure Requirements in U.S. GAAP and IFRSs*, No. 2011-04, May 2011. As of August 13, 2013:
http://www.fasb.org/cs/BlobServer?blobcol=urldata&blobtable=MungoBlobs&blobkey=id&blobwhere=1175822486936&blobheader=application/pdf

Financial Crisis Inquiry Commission, *The Financial Crisis Inquiry Report: Final Report of the National Commission on the Causes of the Financial and Economic Crisis in the United States*, Washington, D.C.: Financial Crisis Inquiry Commission, January 2011. As of August 7, 2013:
http://fcic-static.law.stanford.edu/cdn_media/fcic-reports/fcic_final_report_full.pdf

Financial Services Roundtable, "Comment Letter to FASB re: Accounting for Financial Instruments and Revisions to the Accounting for Derivative Instruments and Hedging Activities," File Reference Number 1810-100, FASB Comment Letter #191, August 13, 2010.

Forbes, Steve, "Steve: End Mark-to-Market," Forbes.com, March 23, 2009.

Freixas, X., B. Parigi, and J.C. Rochet, "Liquidity Provision by the Central Bank," *Journal of Money, Credit and Banking*, Vol. 32, 2000, pp. 611–638.

Gingrich, Newt, "Suspend Mark-to-Market Now!" Forbes.com, September 29, 2008. As of August 7, 2013: http://www.forbes.com/2008/09/29/mark-to-market-oped-cx_ng_0929gingrich.html

Goldman Sachs, "Comment Letter to FASB re: Accounting for Financial Instruments and Revisions to the Accounting for Derivative Instruments and Hedging Activities," File Reference Number 1810-100, FASB Comment Letter #259, September 1, 2010a.

———, "Comment Letter to FASB re: Accounting for Financial Instruments and Revisions to the Accounting for Derivative Instruments and Hedging Activities," File Reference Number 1810-100, FASB Comment Letter #1402, September 30, 2010b.

Heaton, John, Deborah Lucas, and Robert McDonald, "Is Mark-to-Market Accounting Destabilizing? Analysis and Implications for Policy," *Journal of Monetary Economics*, Vol. 57, No. 1, 2008, pp. 64–75.

Hellwig, M. "Systemic Risk in the Financial Sector: An Analysis of the Subprime-Mortgage Financial Crisis," *De Economist*, Vol. 157, 2009, pp. 129–207.

Huizinga, Harry, and Luc A. Laeven, *Bank Valuation and Regulatory Forbearance During a Financial Crisis*, European Banking Center Discussion Paper No. 2009-17, 2010.

International Accounting Standards Board and US-Based Financial Accounting Standards Board, "Memorandum of Understanding: A Roadmap for Convergence Between IFRSs and US GAAP—2006–2008," February 27, 2006. As of August 7, 2013: http://www.fasb.org/cs/BlobServer?blobcol=urldata&blobtable=MungoBlobs&blobkey=id&blobwhere=1175819018800&blobheader=application%2Fpdf

———, *Progress Report on IASB-FASB Convergence Work*, April 21, 2011. As of August 7, 2013: http://www.fasb.org/cs/BlobServer?blobcol=urldata&blobtable=MungoBlobs&blobkey=id&blobwhere=1175822338795&blobheader=application%2Fpdf

Isaac, William M., *Senseless Panic: How Washington Failed America*, Hoboken, N.J.: John Wiley and Sons, 2009a.

———, testimony before the Subcommittee on Capital Markets, Insurance, and Government Sponsored Enterprises, Committee on Financial Services, U.S. House of Representatives, March 12, 2009b.

Johnson, Sarah, and Maria Leone, "Congress Members Fume at Fair Value: Lawmakers Bear Down on FASB Chairman Robert Herz to Modify Fair-Value Rules," CFO.com, March 12, 2009. As of August 7, 2013: http://www.cfo.com/article.cfm/13306816

Journal of Accountancy, "FASB, IASB Chiefs Agree New Convergence Model Is Needed," 2011. As of August 7, 2013: http://www.journalofaccountancy.com/Web/20114869.htm

Kahn, U., "Does Fair Value Accounting Contribute to Systemic Risk in the Banking Industry?" working paper, 2010.

Laux, C., and C. Leuz, "The Crisis of Fair Value Accounting: Making Sense of the Recent Debate," *Accounting, Organizations and Society*, Vol. 34, 2009, pp. 826–834.

———, "Did Fair Value Accounting Contribute to the Financial Crisis?" *Journal of Economic Perspectives*, Vol. 24, No. 1, 2010, pp. 93–118.

McLean, Bethany, and Joe Nocera, *All the Devils Are Here: The Hidden History of the Financial Crisis*, New York: Penguin, 2010.

Merrill, Craig B., Taylor D. Nadauld, Rene M. Stulz, and Shane Sherlund, "Did Capital Requirements and Fair Value Accounting Spark Fire Sales in Distressed Mortgage Securities?" working paper, 2012.

Nissim, Doron, and Stephen Penman, "Principles for the Application of Fair Value Accounting," Center for Excellence in Accounting and Security Analysis, Columbia University Business School White Paper #2, 2010.

Plantin, Guillaume, Haresh Sapra, and Hyun Song Shin, "Marking to Market, Liquidity and Financial Stability," working paper, 2005.

Posen, Robert C., "Is It Fair to Blame Fair Value Accounting for the Financial Crisis?" *Harvard Business Review*, Vol. 87, No. 11, 2010, pp. 84–92.

Public Law 73-66, Banking Act of 1933, June 16, 1933.

Public Law 73-291, Securities and Exchange Act of 1934, June 6, 1934.

Public Law 79-404, Administrative Procedures Act, June 11, 1946.

Public Law 96-221, Institutions Deregulation and Monetary Control Act of 1980, March 31, 1980.

Public Law 97-320, Garn–St. Germain Depository Institutions Act of 1982, October 15, 1982.

Public Law 101-73, Financial Institutions Reform, Recovery and Reinforcement Act of 1989, August 9, 1989.

Public Law 110-343, Emergency Economic Stabilization Act of 2008, October 3, 2008.

Rapoport, M., "'Toxic' Assets Still Lurking at Banks," *Wall Street Journal*, February 7, 2011.

Reinhart, Carmen M., and Kenneth S. Rogoff, *This Time Is Different: Eight Centuries of Financial Folly*, Princeton, N.J.: Princeton University Press, 2008.

Renders, A., "Changing Fair Value Accounting," *Financial Forum*, Vol. 3, No. 2, 2009, pp. 152–155.

Roberts, Russell, *Gambling with Other People's Money: How Perverted Incentives Caused the Financial Crisis*, Washington, D.C.: Mercatus Center, George Mason University, 2010. As of August 7, 2013:
http://mercatus.org/sites/default/files/publication/RUSS-final.pdf

Sapra, Haresh, "Do Accounting Measurement Regimes Matter? A Discussion of Mark-to-Market Accounting and Liquidity Pricing," *Journal of Accounting and Economics*, Vol. 45, 2008, pp. 379–387.

Schwarcz, Steven L., "Systemic Risk," *Georgetown Law Journal*, Vol. 97, 2008, pp. 193–249.

SEC—*See* U.S. Securities and Exchange Commission.

Senior Supervisors Group, *Observations on Risk Management Practices During the Recent Market Turbulence*, 2008. As of August 7, 2013:
http://www.newyorkfed.org/newsevents/news/banking/2008/SSG_Risk_Mgt_doc_final.pdf

———, *Risk Management Lessons from the Global Banking Crisis of 2008*, 2009. As of August 7, 2013:
http://www.sec.gov/news/press/2009/report102109.pdf

Shaffer, Sanders, "Fair Value Accounting: Villain or Innocent Victim: Exploring the Links Between Fair Value Accounting, Bank Regulatory Capital and the Recent Financial Crisis," Federal Reserve Bank of Boston, Working Paper No. QAU10-01, 2010.

Shearer, Jana, "Mark-to-Market: Delivering the Financial Crisis to Your Front Door," *Ohio Northern Law Review*, Vol. 36, 2010, pp. 236–261.

Smith, Chandy, *An Overview of Outreach Provided Through Meetings and Teleconferences with Users of Financial Statements for the FASB's Accounting for Financial Instruments Proposal*, Financial Accounting Standards Board, September 29, 2010. As of August 13, 2013:
http://www.fasb.org/cs/ContentServer?site=FASB&c=Document_C&pagename=FASB%2FDocument_C%2F DocumentPage&cid=1176157524718

Story, Louise, Landon Thomas Jr., and Nelson D. Shwartz, "Wall St. Helped to Mask Debt Fueling Europe's Crisis," *New York Times*, February 13, 2010.

U.S. Department of the Treasury, Office of the Comptroller of the Currency, "Risk-Based Capital Guidelines; Capital Adequacy Guidelines; Capital Maintenance: Regulatory Capital; Impact of Modifications to Generally Accepted Accounting Principles; Consolidation of Asset-Backed Commercial Paper Programs; and Other Related Issues," *Federal Register*, Vol. 75, No. 18, January 28, 2010, p. 4636.

U.S. Federal Reserve, *The Federal Reserve System: Purposes and Functions*, Washington, D.C., 2005. As of August 7, 2013:
http://www.federalreserve.gov/pf/pdf/pf_complete.pdf

U.S. General Accounting Office, *Failed Banks: Accounting and Auditing Reforms Urgently Needed*, Washington, D.C., GAO/AFMD 91-43, 1991. As of August 7, 2013:
http://www.gao.gov/assets/160/150382.pdf

———, *Resolution Trust Corporation's 1995 and 1994 Financial Statements*, GAO/AIMD-96-123, Washington, D.C., 1996. As of August 7, 2013:
http://www.gao.gov/assets/230/222902.pdf

U.S. Securities and Exchange Commission, Office of the Chief Accountant, Division of Corporation Finance, *Report and Recommendations Pursuant to Section 133 of the Emergency Economic Stabilization Act of 2008: Study on Mark-to-Market Accounting*, Washington D.C., 2008. As of August 7, 2013:
http://www.sec.gov/news/studies/2008/marktomarket123008.pdf

White, Lawrence J., *The S&L Debacle: Public Policy Lessons for Bank and Thrift Regulation*, New York: Oxford University Press, 1991.